Gentile *Girl*

Living with the
Latter-day Saints

D1472573

Carol Avery Forseth

Gentile Girl: Living with the Latter-day Saints

Unless otherwise noted, Scripture taken from the New American
Standard Bible, Copyright The Lockman Foundation 1960, 1962, 1963,
1968, 1971, 1972, 1973, 1975, 1977, 1995. Used by permission.
(www.lockman.org)

Other Scripture references, as noted, are from the King James Version
of the Bible.

The Scripture quotations in Appendix B marked (NIV) are taken from
the HOLY BIBLE, NEW INTERNATIONAL VERSION ®.
Copyright © 1973, 1978, 1984 by International Bible Society. Used by
permission of Zondervan. All rights reserved.

ISBN 0-9714782-0-1

Library of Congress Control Number: 2001096118

As noted in the epilogue, an earlier version of this story was published
in 1989 as *Faith under Fire: Living with the Latter-day Saints*.

Crossroads Press
P.O. Box 272817
Fort Collins, Colorado 80527-2817

www.gentilegirl.com
www.crossroadspress.net

Crossroads
Press
Fort Collins, Colorado

"A young Christian girl ventures into a beautiful but strange land—a land where even Jews are Gentiles."

*J*anet urged me to accept this challenge from her and from God with an open mind. She pledged that if I found it to be untrue, she and millions of Saints would leave the Church.

She closed with this: "I promise you, dear sister, that if you pray to God with an open mind and ask Him if what I have said is true, you will have a good feeling come over you and the Holy Ghost will bear witness to its truthfulness...I also guarantee that you will never rest the same if you deny the feelings you receive...Now the weight is on you to test it and prove it to yourself."

chapter one

I was seventeen years old and wondering where to go to college. In October, I spent an afternoon at a high school seniors' fair. After three hours of talking with eager recruiters and collecting a load of information packets, I was ready to go home.

On my way to the parking lot, I passed one more door marked, "Brigham Young University, Provo, Utah."

"Why not," I thought. "As long as I'm here." I opened the door.

The recruiter inside was blond, clean-cut, and overdressed for the occasion. He asked me what I knew about Brigham Young University.

"Not a thing. I was just on my way home."

He handed me an information packet. Noticing my armload of material, he said, "You look tired. Why don't you sit down and watch this short video?"

I sank into a chair, glad to get off my feet. The film explained that Brigham Young University, located in a spectacular mountain valley, was supported and operated by the Church of Jesus Christ of Latter-day Saints—the "Mormons." BYU offered hundreds of majors in more than a dozen colleges. When the film ended, I had a couple of questions.

"I'm going to study music. I play the French horn," I said. "What do you know about the music department?"

"I studied music too, as a horn player! Our School of Music is well known for excellence in music performance, composition, and education. Our performing groups travel around the U.S. and even internationally."

"Sounds wonderful, but I'm not a Mormon," I confessed. "Can I still attend your school?"

"Of course! Students of all religions attend BYU. We accept any qualified student who agrees to abide by the standards of the University and the Church. You'll find the Honor Code in your materials. Tuition rates are slightly higher for non-LDS students because the Church finances seventy percent of the University budget. Church members get a break because they've been tithing all their lives, but the rates you pay as a non-member are still lower than you'd pay at any other private institution."

As I filled out an information card, the recruiter said, "If your grades are good, you ought to apply for a scholarship. I don't usually give away catalogs, but here, I'd like you to have one. I hope you will consider attending our university."

That evening I sorted through my stacks of material and found the Code of Honor that all students were required to sign. Students agreed to be honest, chaste, virtuous, and law-abiding. They were expected to use clean language, to show respect for others, and to abstain from alcoholic beverages, tobacco, tea, coffee, and other harmful substances. All students and staff were to observe the dress and grooming code, calling for a clean and well-maintained appearance. No wonder the guy was dressed like that.

Sounded good so far. I wanted to be around law-abiding people of high morals, clean language, and modest dress. I liked structure. I could live without tea and coffee. I had heard of the Mormon Tabernacle Choir, and I knew Mormons were big on family life and missionary activity. As for the rest of it, I wasn't much interested in Mormonism or any other religion.

The next week during a Phoenix Youth Symphony rehearsal, I remembered that my friend Sheryl in the horn section was Mormon. We'd shared a hotel room at a music workshop, and I'd seen her reading a Mormon book. Sheryl was petite and frilly; she always reminded me of Little Bo Peep, but when she played her horn she sounded like a six-foot muscle man. At the break, I told her about my visit with the Brigham Young University recruiter.

Sheryl clapped her hands and actually bounced up

and down. "Guess what! I'm planning to go to BYU too! Wouldn't it be fun to go together?"

"Well, I haven't made up my mind yet."

"Provo is beautiful. I've been there before and I've met the horn teacher. He plays principal horn in the Utah Symphony." Sheryl cocked her head sideways. "You're not LDS, are you? What sect do you belong to?"

"Sect? I don't know. I don't attend church much. I'm a Christian, I guess."

"Oh, that's okay. Mormons are Christians too. The real name of our church is the Church of Jesus Christ of Latter-day Saints. Did you know that I used to be a Methodist? About four years ago my family joined the Church, and it has changed our lives! If you come to BYU, you'll have a chance to see what it's all about."

That night I told my parents that Sheryl was going to BYU.

"You seem pretty interested in this," my mother said. "Why don't you go see Mr. Bradford at school? High school counselors have all kinds of information about college."

When I went to see Mr. Bradford, he said, "Brigham Young University? I did graduate work there. I'd be happy to write you a recommendation. I have applications for admission and for scholarships right here."

I decided to send in the forms. It was almost December, and the pressure was on to decide about college. I hated making big decisions, and applying to BYU was one small step I could take.

At home, meanwhile, my fifteen-year-old sister Nancy had been visiting a Baptist church with a friend. She was, in my father's words, "getting churchy." As my mom said, Nancy was always the sensitive one in the family. My older brother Mark let his snide opinion be known, but I didn't care where Nancy went to church as long as she didn't bother me with it. Todd, my younger brother, was only eleven, so he still did whatever he was told.

Then Mom announced that the family was going to visit the Baptist church with Nancy to show our broad-minded support. On Sunday, Mom and Dad and the kids went to see what the "Bible bangers" were like. They didn't bang on the Bible but they did read it, and there were Bibles in the pews.

While they passed the offering plate, I picked up a pew Bible and opened it in the middle. The words at the top of the page caught my attention: "He, your Teacher, will no longer hide himself, but your eyes will behold your Teacher. And your ears will hear a word behind you, 'This is the way, walk in it,' whenever you turn to the right or to the left" (Isaiah 30:20-21, NASB).

I read the words again and thought, "Hear a voice

from a Teacher? I wonder if that voice would tell me where to go to school next year."

I didn't keep going back to church, but my sister did, and one night she breezed into the house saying she had "accepted Christ" and was going to be baptized. Now this was too much for me. It's not that I hated religion, but I had always imagined God up in the sky minding His own business while I minded mine. I thought that as long as I made good use of the talents He gave me and tried to live a good life, God would be satisfied even if I wasn't the pious type.

But I had wondered about "hearing a voice behind me" and I remembered that Baptist preacher's sermon. He said each person had to *accept* salvation. I had never given much thought before to eternal life; I guess I thought everyone was "saved."

Also, my sister seemed different since her "conversion." We couldn't make her mad as easily as before, and she seemed eager to read the Bible and go to church. My parents and siblings saw it too, and they decided to go back to church with her.

"Not me!" I declared on Sunday morning. "I've had enough religion!"

I stayed home trying to forget about religion, but I couldn't. What if everyone did have to accept or reject God? I was a busy girl—not interested in joining a church, but on the other hand, I wasn't about to reject God. I was just afraid of where all this religion might lead me.

My mother and father and brothers charged into the house after church. "Guess what, Carol!" my mother said. She looked like she had been crying. "We accepted Christ into our lives this morning! They gave an invitation, and we each decided to receive Christ. The Bible says we've become children of God! We're going back tonight to talk with the pastor about being baptized as a family."

I started to cry. Now I was at a fork in the road. Was my whole family going to do this without me? I decided not to take any chances. I joined the family that evening and talked with the pastor. It seemed God gave me the words to awkwardly pray, "Dear God, I can't choose against You. You sent Jesus to die on the cross for me. I give my life to you." We Averys: father, mother, older brother, younger sister, younger brother, and I were baptized together that very evening and joined the North Phoenix Baptist Church.

I was surprised to wake up the next morning feeling joyful. I *wanted* to read the Bible. I *wanted* to tell people that I believed in Jesus. This was not normal. I was pretty self-centered by nature. I went back to school and felt compassion for the outcast "nerdy" kids and for the teacher who usually got on my nerves. My school friends said, "Something's different about you."

Now that I had this new life with God I began to wonder whether BYU was the place for me. I asked my Sunday school teacher what she thought. "Carol! Surely you're not serious! You're a new believer! Those Mormons would try to convert you. You'd better *not* go to BYU!"

Every week at orchestra rehearsal, Sheryl and I had lively conversations about BYU. We felt so grown up, talking about going off to college and living in the dormitory. Sheryl was sure I would love BYU and promised that we could be roommates. BYU did seem safe; at least with the Honor Code there wouldn't be a lot of drinking and drugs.

One night Sheryl said, "Carol, next week our ward is having an open house. Would you and your family like to be my guests?"

"Your ward?" I asked.

"Yes, that's our congregation. The Church is divided into wards, and we all attend the ward closest to our house."

My family, still broad-minded, came along in support, and we met Sheryl, her mom, and her brother at the ward meetinghouse. Inside the building was a gymnasium full of tables crammed with food. Sheryl proudly introduced us to her bishop, the leader of her ward. She explained that LDS bishops are volunteer church members.

After dinner, we watched a short movie called "Meet the Mormons" and then joined a walking tour of the building led by two perfectly groomed young men whose nametags identified them as "Elder Brown" and "Elder Benson." Elder Brown directed our attention to a series of large paintings along a hallway.

He switched on a light under a portrait of a nineteenth-century youth with a bow tied around his neck. "I would like to begin by sharing the testimony of Joseph Smith, whom our Heavenly Father sent to restore Christ's Church in the latter days." Elder Brown explained that during a religious revival in 1820, Joseph had been invited to join many churches, but didn't know which one to join. While he was praying in the woods, two "embodied personages" appeared to Joseph. The first, God the Father, pointed to the other and said, "This is my beloved Son. Hear him!" The personages told Joseph to join none of the churches, for they were all wrong.

According to Elder Brown, Joseph continued praying, and three years later an angel of light appeared to him. The angel introduced himself as Moroni, a messenger of God, and he directed Joseph to a hill near his home. Buried there was a religious history that prophets of an ancient American civilization had engraved onto golden plates. With the help of two special seers' stones, Joseph translated the golden plates into English as the Book of Mormon, which was first published in 1830.

Now Elder Benson spoke. "While translating the Book of Mormon, Joseph Smith and his scribe, Oliver

Cowdery, were in the woods praying. Suddenly three of the original apostles, Peter, James and John, appeared and bestowed upon them the authority to restore the true Church upon the earth, which had been lost after the last original apostle died.

"Joseph did as he was commanded and established the Church of Jesus Christ of Latter-day Saints. As in Jesus' day, it was to be directed by apostles and prophets who received revelation from the risen Christ. Since that time a living prophet has always been on earth to reveal to us truths that are vital to our salvation. When we follow the prophet's counsel, we can be assured of blessings from the Lord."

Elder Brown spoke again. "I would like to conclude our presentation by bearing testimony to you of the truth of these things. I know God lives, that Jesus is the Christ, and that they are separate beings of flesh and bone. I testify that these two did come to earth and appear to Joseph Smith and that this is the true Church. I say these things in the name of Jesus Christ. Amen."

I lay awake that night thinking about our visit to the ward. The Mormons put on a good show: nice building, good cooking, friendly people. But what a story: angels of light, golden plates buried in the ground, modern prophets! And they said that every church but their own was false, even the church I'd just joined.

So what was I to do? I wanted to go to BYU, but I

didn't want to become a Mormon. I liked the Honor Code, but what if the Church influence was too strong? Sheryl was my friend; surely she would look out for me. On the other hand, she probably wanted to convert me. But among twenty-five thousand students, there'd have to be a few of my kind of Christians.

I talked with the pastor at my new church. He said, "Mormons are very persuasive; they'll try to convert you. But maybe God has a special plan for you there. I'm sure He can use a willing Christian in a place like that. Keep praying about it."

The next week I was offered a four-year full-tuition scholarship to BYU. I accepted.

chapter two

I decided to attend a freshman seminar one week before school started. It was worth a semester credit and might give me a chance to make friends and learn my way around the university. In August my dad and I packed our station wagon full and got ready to leave for Provo.

My mother said, "Carol, we've raised you to be sensible. Now we place you in God's hands. You may be pressured by those Mormons, but whatever you do, we're behind you one hundred percent." My mother was always behind me one hundred percent.

"Oh, Mom, you don't think I'm going to become a Mormon, do you?"

"We will love you no matter what, but don't stay there if you are miserable, okay? Call us collect if you need anything. And remember, God will take care of you."

I hugged her and said goodbye to my sister and brothers, and Dad and I got in the car. As we drove away, I watched and waved until I could no longer see them. My dad was the strong, silent type. I knew he loved me—he often said so—but he didn't have too much else to say.

I was glad for the quiet ride, because I was an introvert too, especially when I had a lot on my mind. Now that we were on our way, I felt afraid. I wondered if it was too late to back out. Had I passed the point of no return? Maybe I should have gone to Arizona State instead. I kept my thoughts to myself, and Dad kept driving toward Utah.

We ended our long drive at a motel outside Provo. The next morning, Dad and I checked the phonebook and found an address for the First Baptist Church. We stopped by, but the church was locked up. Peering in the window, I saw a small sanctuary with fifteen or twenty rows of pews. "Looks small," I said to my dad. "Our church in Phoenix is way bigger than this."

We drove to the "Y" (as Mormons affectionately call their campus) and began to explore on foot. Even the grass sparkled in the brilliant sunshine. The grounds were perfectly manicured, and the buildings looked polished. Flowers and fountains adorned the sidewalks.

We entered the Harris Fine Arts Center, home of the music department. The glass doors opened into a three-story atrium and art gallery with a concert hall at one end and a theater at the other. Our steps echoed throughout the gallery as we walked down the marble staircase. In the basement, music practice rooms lined the hallways.

We checked out Helaman Halls, the dormitory complex I would move into after the first week. The rooms were cozy; the bathrooms were down the hall. We dropped off some suitcases for storage. Over lunch Dad taught me how to balance my brand-new checking account, and then it was time to check in for the seminar.

I told the registrar my name. "Carol Avery? Let me see." She squinted hard at her papers. "There's no Carol; on this list we have a 'Card Avery.' Card Avery? Oh no, they put you in the boys' dorm!" She left in a hurry.

I turned around and apologized to the person behind me in line, but the registrar soon returned and said, "It's okay. We've put you in the girls' dorm now, seventh floor. Here's your key."

Now I was sure there was no turning back. Dad and I carried my suitcases to the seventh floor, had a look at the room, and walked back to the car together.

"I guess that's all, then," he said as he hugged me. "God bless you, daughter." "Take care. We'll miss you."

I couldn't look straight at him because the tears were ready to fall. "Bye, Dad. I'll write. See you at Christmas. I love you." One more hug and he was gone. I waved and turned back toward the dormitory.

My roommate hadn't arrived yet. As I unpacked my first suitcase, I heard a knock on the door. "Come in," I called.

"Hi, I'm Linda. I live next door." Linda was a conversational genius; we chatted about our hometowns and our families and our majors in rapid succession and suddenly Linda asked me, "Are you Mormon?"

My heart skipped a beat. "No," I answered, "why do you ask?"

"Well, neither am I, and I don't intend to become one."

"No kidding! Are you a Christian?"

"Yes, of course. Hey, these Mormons have some crazy ideas. Have you heard they used to practice polygamy? And they are prejudiced toward Blacks. It's in their doctrines. I want to make friends here but forget about joining their Church."

"I've heard those doctrines too. Linda, I'm very glad to meet you. I asked God for some non-Mormon friends."

Finally, late in the afternoon, my roommate Wendy showed up. Wendy was tall, neither fat nor thin, and her brown bangs were held back by one of those wide stretchy hair bands. Once she was settled, I told Wendy all about myself, except for my big secret: I wasn't Mormon.

At dinnertime, we sat with a group of girls in the cafeteria; they talked excitedly, but I didn't say much. I listened and tried to understand. Some of them had boyfriends who were at the LTM[1] preparing to go to exotic places like Korea and Peru. Many of the girls had been active in "Relief Society"—it sounded like the Red Cross, but turned out to be the women's organization of the Church.[2] The girls were hoping to hear some General Authorities[3] speak at devotionals in the Marriott Center, BYU's indoor arena.

Clearly Mormonism was more than religion for these people—it was a culture, a way of life. I was an outsider and I couldn't fake it forever. That night I decided to break the news to Wendy. I watched her unpack, waited for the right moment, and finally said the words, "Wendy, I'm not a Mormon."

"You're not?" She stopped putting clothes away and stared at me, amazed. "What are you?"

"I'm a Christian."

"Well, so am I."

"I'm a Baptist."

"Oh. What are you doing here?"

"It's a good school, and I got a scholarship. I prayed about it."

Wendy invited me to come with her to the ward on Sunday.

The next morning at orientation, one of the leaders asked who knew how to lead music. Of course I did; I was a music major, so I raised my hand.

"Great! Come on up! We'll start off this morning with some hymn singing."

Hymns? I didn't know any Mormon hymns! I wasn't about to back down in front of everyone, though. There were some hymnals scattered on the chairs, so I grabbed one and walked to the front.

"What should we sing?" I asked.

Someone called out "We Thank Thee, O God, for a Prophet" and another student called out the page number. The pianist played an introduction.

I directed with my eyes fixed on the hymnal while everyone sang. When I glanced up, I saw that most people weren't using a hymnal at all. The next request was "Praise to the Man Who Communed with Jehovah," another hymn about Joseph Smith. We ended with "Come, Come Ye Saints," a beautiful hymn about courage in hard times. Then the program director stood to make opening remarks, and I sat down in relief.

We were dismissed to our classes; with a major in music and a minor in Spanish, I had registered for the humanities survey. Our professor's first question was, "Is anyone here not LDS?"

I was the only one to raise my hand. "Welcome to BYU. I'm sure you'll be able to contribute much to our discussions," said Brother Greene. Brother Greene was tall and thin; he looked like he preferred reading books to eating meals. We called all our authority figures Brother or Sister So-and-So.

Our study of humanities included the history of religion, and I worried about that topic. I had never studied the history of any religion, much less the Latter-day Saints, and I had only been reading the Bible for a few months. Class participation was part of our grade, so I strove to answer any "safe" questions that came along.

Linda and I turned out to be the only non-Mormons in the whole group. Linda knew most everyone by name within three days, and she spoke her mind about the Church. I was friendly to everyone but I felt very alone and overwhelmed on the inside. The other students were curious about me. They referred to me, and to every non-Mormon, as a Gentile. (Even Jews were Gentiles!)

I learned something new about Latter-day Saints every day, like in the cafeteria, when a girl asked me, "Why do you wear a cross?"

"I like to. It reminds me of what Christ did for me." Suddenly I realized I had seen no crosses at BYU.

"We don't believe in the cross. We prefer to emphasize the life of our Savior. To us, worshipping the cross is idol worship."

I had worn my cross necklace every day. I might as well have worn a sign saying, "I'm not LDS; I'm an idol worshipper."

Back in my room, I looked up "cross" in my Bible concordance. I read 1 Corinthians 1:18, "For the word of the cross is to those who are perishing foolishness, but to us who are being saved it is the power of God." (NASB)

Should I stop wearing my cross? I wasn't ashamed of it, but did I want to announce to everyone that I was not LDS? I did not. I decided to put my cross away, and I wore my Christian fish necklace instead.

All week long my classmates invited me to attend Sunday's Sacrament Meeting. I didn't have transportation to the Baptist church anyway, so on Sunday I went along to the 36th Branch meeting. All BYU students were assigned to branches according to where they lived; branches were like LDS wards but met on campus in classroom buildings. Several branches formed a "stake;" wards were organized into stakes in the same way.

I dared to sit next to my classmate Bruce. He was handsome and obviously smart; he knew all the answers in class, and I'd felt the intensity of his ice-blue eyes on me the rare times I spoke up. I felt drawn to him and yet reserved around him.

The Sacrament Meeting began with singing and prayer. Then the sacrament was passed, first bread and then water. I tried to act reverent as I passed them along without participating.

There was no minister to preach a sermon; instead three students each gave fifteen-minute talks. The first two talks focused on moral principles and right living. Then a tiny shy girl from our group told her personal story. She could barely see over the podium and spoke in a voice so quiet the audience strained to listen. She had been raised in an abusive home and rejected by her parents. Her family never went to church. When she was in high school, an LDS classmate befriended her and introduced her to the local missionaries. She took the series of lessons they offered, became convinced of the truth of the Church, and wanted to be baptized. Her parents refused to allow it, and attending BYU was out of the question. She saved her money, waited for her eighteenth birthday, and was now at BYU for her first semester. With tears flowing, she expressed her love for the Church and her gratitude to the Lord for revealing to her the truth of the gospel.

By now, listeners across the room were sniffling and wiping their eyes. Bruce leaned over to me and whispered, "What a strong testimony she has!"

I shrugged and smiled.

"Oh, I forgot you're a non-member."

After another hymn and prayer, the meeting ended. The moderator announced that after a short break, there would be a fireside for the seminar students.

"A fireside?" I asked Bruce.

"We usually have them on Sunday nights," he said. "Another speaker and refreshments. Nothing to do with a fire. By the way, what religion are you?"

"I'm a Christian—a Baptist."

Bruce said, "Carol, what do you believe about the Godhead?"

"The Godhead? Is that the same as the Trinity?"

"We don't believe in the Trinity. We believe God has a body of flesh and bone, immortal and intangible, and so does His Son, Jesus Christ. Together with the Holy Ghost, these are three separate and distinct personages."

"Oh." We sat down as the fireside was about to begin, and one of the leaders asked me to lead singing again. After a couple of hymns, an academic dean gave a talk about virtuous living at the University. I couldn't disagree with those good moral principles, though the speaker quoted LDS books. But I was getting exhausted from listening to talks and trying to sort out what I believed.

The speaker mentioned a group of people called Lamanites. He said, "I'm not critical of them. In fact, maybe some of you are Lamanites." I wondered what a Lamanite might be, and whether I was one.

Bruce walked me back to the dorm, and I asked him, "Am I a Lamanite?"

Bruce laughed aloud and exclaimed, "I don't think so! The Lamanites were ancient inhabitants of the American continent. The Book of Mormon contains the record of two peoples, the fair-skinned Nephites and the dark-skinned Lamanites. In the end, all the Nephites were killed and the

Lamanites survived. Their descendants are the Native Americans, whom we call Lamanites."

"I'm not a Lamanite." I decided to ask another question, since Bruce seemed so well informed. I had heard of the word Zion in the Bible, but since coming to Provo I'd seen Zion's National Bank and Zion's Cooperative Mercantile Institution (a department store known as ZCMI). "Why are things named Zion around here?"

Bruce answered, "Zion is the city of God. It's where the saints of God dwell. Utah is called Zion because this is where the Latter-day Saints finally settled."

We reached the dormitory and sat on a bench overlooking the lights of the campus. "Carol," Bruce asked after some silence, "why did you come here?"

I explained, and Bruce said, "So you don't know much about the Church. Would you like to know more?"

Enough should have been enough by then, but I was too polite to say no. "I guess."

"There are many verses in the Bible that most Christians ignore, but we take seriously—for example, 1 Corinthians 15:29. Here, read it."

I read from Bruce's King James Version, "Else what shall they do which are baptized for the dead, if the dead rise not at all? Why are they then baptized for the dead?" I had no idea what that meant.

Bruce said, "We Latter-day Saints baptize for the

dead, like this verse says. Since baptism is essential to enter the Celestial Kingdom, everyone deserves the chance to be baptized. But what about all the people who never heard the true gospel—who lived before the restoration of the Church? God is loving and fair, and we believe He gives everyone a chance to be saved. Based on 1 Peter 3, these people will hear the gospel after they die. Here."

Reluctantly I read again from his Bible, "For Christ preached unto the spirits in prison; which sometime were disobedient, when once the longsuffering of God waited in the days of Noah, while the ark was a preparing, wherein few, that is, eight souls were saved by water."

Bruce explained, "So Christ preaches to the people who have died, but even if they believe, they still need to be baptized. We Latter-day Saints have accepted the task of tracing our genealogy to find names of people who were not baptized into the Church. It's a huge job, but with God's help, we can eventually baptize everyone who has ever lived on earth. Jesus said, 'Be ye therefore perfect,' and we believe that we can be."

I had reached my limit, but Bruce was on a roll. "Carol, what do you think of the Book of Mormon?"

I answered, "I haven't read it, but I don't believe it is Scripture." I used one of the few Bible verses I knew on him. "In Revelation it says never to add or take away from the Word of God."

"Oh, yes. I know that passage. But it only refers to the Book of Revelation itself. Or it might be a mistranslation. The Bible has passed through so many hands, especially after the True Apostolic Church was lost from the earth, that it has many errors. Joseph Smith began translating an Inspired Version of the Bible, but he was martyred before he finished it. Fortunately we have modern-day Scriptures to complement the Bible.

"Carol, the Book of Mormon contains much wisdom, and if you read it, God will reveal the truth to you. Are you afraid to read it?"

"No, I'm not afraid. But I'm exhausted." I stood up. "I'm going now. Thank you for walking me home."

As I climbed the stairs to my dorm room, I was glad for a break from Bruce. He made my head ache. I hoped I wouldn't see him after this seminar was over.

When I opened my door, some girls were sitting on the floor laughing and talking with Wendy, my roommate. They greeted me cheerfully, but I couldn't bear to sit down and act happy. Tired of being around people, I took my Bible and left.

I wanted to be alone, but I couldn't go outside. It was 11:30 p.m., and the dormitory doors would get locked at midnight. I'd have to ask the resident assistant to let me back in. I went down to the laundry room in the basement, which was locked to prevent students from washing clothes on Sundays. I slumped to the basement floor, leaned against the door, and cried.

"Help, Lord," I prayed. "I'm so tired. I can't make sense of all this Mormon teaching. I don't understand those verses Bruce showed me. Why are they in the Bible anyway? What are they supposed to mean? Please help me understand. I feel so alone."

I leafed desperately through my Bible and spotted 1 Corinthians 10:13, a verse I'd underlined: "No temptation has overtaken you but such as is common to man; and God is faithful, who will not allow you to be tempted beyond what you are able, but with the temptation will provide the way of escape also, that you may be able to endure it." (NASB) I was comforted as the warm tears rolled down my cheeks.

We had a couple of days off before the fall semester started. While moving my luggage to Helaman Halls, I saw Linda, the other Gentile from my seminar.

"Linda!" I shouted across the parking lot. "Wait a minute!"

She stopped for me. "Looks like you're moving into Helaman Halls too," she said.

"Yes. I hope to see you sometimes. I'm tired of being around all Mormons."

"Not me," she said. "I'm having a great time! Have you been to any Church meetings yet? I like them a lot."

"I went to Church meetings all day Sunday. They wore me out."

"Not me."

When I was unpacking that evening, Linda stopped by my new room. "Hey, there's a testimony meeting tonight. I'm going. Want to come?"

"No, thanks. My roommate should be here tomorrow, and I'm not done unpacking."

"Okay. Bye!" She was gone.

Linda was making lots of friends at BYU and having a great time. I was trying to make friends too, but was it possible to fit in here without joining the Church? I wondered.

I could hardly wait for Sheryl to arrive. When I came back from lunch the next day the door to my dorm room was open. I rushed in to say hi, but it wasn't Sheryl. A strange man was sitting on my bed. A woman carrying a small child was unpacking a box. Two boys walked into the room carrying another big box. They stopped when they saw me. A girl about my height wearing wire-rimmed glasses strode in behind them.

"Hi, are you Carol? I'm Janet Merrill, your roommate. These are my parents, and that's Julie, my little sister. These are my brothers, Robert and John."

"Hello. Something's wrong. My roommate is Sheryl

Stevens from Phoenix."

"This is G2204, isn't it? It's my assigned room, and they said my roommate's name is Carol." She straightened her glasses on her nose.

"Oh, no!" I thought. "Another mix-up." I didn't have the confidence to tackle the problem right then; I was sure Sheryl would come find me, and we'd straighten it all out. "Do you need help?" I asked.

"No, all the boxes are up now. Thanks anyway."

Janet's father made room for me to sit down. He cleared his throat, looked at me over the top of his glasses, and asked, "Are you Greek Orthodox?"

"Greek Orthodox? No, I'm Baptist."

Mrs. Merrill pointed to the poster above my bed, a Christian fish symbol with the Greek letters *icthus*,[ΙΧΘΥΣ] the same symbol I wore on my necklace. "We knew it was a religious symbol, and it wasn't LDS. We guessed Greek Orthodox."

Soon Janet and her family went shopping, and I went to look for Sheryl. "Sheryl Stevens?" the desk clerk repeated as she checked her list. "She's in room G2104."

I hurried there and knocked on the door. Sheryl opened the door and rushed out to hug me. "What happened to you?" she asked.

"I've been waiting for you in the room exactly upstairs."

"Oh, no! I've been waiting for you down here! What should we do? Do you like your roommate?"

"She seems nice enough," I said. "How about yours?"

"I don't know. I thought *you* were my roommate. I guess she's not here yet. I just spent hours unpacking and putting everything up on the walls. I was wondering where you were. Oh, what should we do?" Sheryl sat down, stood up, and sat back down again.

"I don't know," I said. "I've unpacked, too. What if they don't let us change rooms?"

"Maybe we could room together next year." Since she suggested it, maybe she didn't want to room with me after all. I didn't feel brave enough to try to change rooms and move all my luggage again, and so there it was: next year.

Janet, Sheryl and I went down to dinner together. Janet said, "You both are music majors! Wow, that's wonderful! I've played piano for my ward. I love music, but I've decided to major in family studies."

"Sheryl's a really good horn player," I said. "Better than me. She was in the All-State Orchestra for three years."

Janet said, "I hope I can come to some of your concerts." Janet was trying hard to be friendly.

That night Janet and I attended dorm orientation in the lobby. The gray-hair-in-a-bun dorm mother passed out several pages of rules.

"Girls, please follow along on your regulation sheets." She discussed each rule and the penalty for breaking it. She reminded us that we had come to BYU by choice, and had agreed to abide by the school's standards.

"Your resident assistant will inspect your rooms once a month." Janet and I made faces at each other.

"Please note the visitation hours. Men are allowed to enter your rooms on alternate Sunday afternoons from 2 to 4 p.m. Your doors are to be left open when men visit your rooms. Otherwise you may visit with male friends in the dorm lobby."

"My boyfriend is in Germany on a mission," Janet whispered, her eyes bright.

"I don't have a boyfriend," I whispered back.

Back in our room, I asked Janet, "What do you think of all the rules?"

"They're pretty strict, but rules help us to obey the commandments of the Lord. They show us the way to obtain exaltation in the Celestial Kingdom."

"What is the Celestial Kingdom? I've heard of that." Bruce had mentioned it. "Does that mean heaven?"

"There are three levels of heaven: the Celestial, the Terrestrial, and the Telestial Kingdoms. It's in the Bible." She picked hers up and flipped the pages. "Here, let me read you 1 Corinthians 15:40-41: 'There are also celestial bodies, and bodies terrestrial: but the glory of the celestial is one, and the glory of the terrestrial is another. There is one glory of the sun, and another glory of the moon, and another glory of the stars: for one star differeth from another star in glory.' So there are three glories.

"We earn our place in one of these three degrees of glory. Most people will go to one of these heavens, except Satan and the apostates. We who keep all the commandments and receive endowments in the temple will go to the Celestial Kingdom, becoming gods and goddesses ourselves. By then our Heavenly Father will have progressed to a higher level, so we never actually catch up with Him. We call it eternal progression. We never stop progressing, nor does Heavenly Father, nor His Heavenly Father..."

Now here was some peculiar theology. "Janet, did you say God has a Heavenly Father?"

"Well, yes. How do you think our Heavenly Father came into being? We only have one God, but God has a Father too, and so on. We know this because of revelation to the latter-day prophets. And our other Scriptures fill in the gaps that the Bible leaves."

"Oh boy, Janet, I've had all the theology I can handle for tonight." I wanted to plug my ears with my fingers.

"Yeah, sorry. I'm sure it's all new to you. Carol, I'm so glad you're my roommate. We can learn a lot from each other. But now we'd better get a good night's sleep.

Tomorrow we start classes!"

We turned out the light, and I thought about Janet. Like Bruce, she sure knew Mormon theology, but she seemed a lot nicer. No doubt she wanted to convert me. But she was not an enemy; she had already become a friend. Was this mix-up God's plan for me?

chapter three

Music theory, my first class, got underway at eight the next morning. To my relief, I was on level ground with my LDS classmates in the study of harmony and melody. The professor, Brother Turner, was short, vigorous, and outgoing. In a charitable move toward his new freshmen, he didn't ask if there were any Gentiles in the class. I liked Brother Turner right away.

After class I went outside and sat beside a shimmering fountain. I couldn't get enough of the sunshine and the crisp mountain air. I watched hundreds of students walk past and wondered which one out of each hundred was not LDS.

"Wow," I thought. "I'm surrounded by Mormons. My roommate is Mormon, my classmates are Mormon, and my teachers are Mormon. I eat Mormon food and sleep in a Mormon bed. I am over my head in an ocean of Mormonism. I've got to get to that Baptist church."

That afternoon I called the number from the phone

book. The pastor's wife answered and offered me a ride for Sunday morning. On Sunday, when we arrived at the Baptist church, she pointed me toward the college class, where a mere four people were seated. Two of them attended Utah Technical College, but John and Gary, the other two, were genuine BYU students. John was blond and short, and Gary was tall and dark. I introduced myself calmly, using self-control to keep from hugging them.

The pastor himself, Don Plott, visited our class to talk about forming a Baptist Student Union at BYU. Pastor Don was sturdy but not fat, with a head full of curly brown hair. "In recent years, we've had so few students it was hard to begin student work. It looks like we might have more this year. Now is the time to get a BSU off the ground.

"After we submit names of student officers to the BYU Organizations Office, we will be recognized as an official club on campus. John, can I put you down as the president?"

"Sure."

Don turned to Gary. "Vice-president?"

"Glad to."

"Now Carol," Don said, "we need one more name. How about secretary-treasurer?"

"Me?" I looked around.

"You're a Baptist, right? You're a BYU student?"

Always one to be helpful and rarely one to say no,

I hardly even hesitated. "Okay. Put me down."

I sat with John and Gary in the small sanctuary. I found out that John Cole, a junior, and Gary Smith, a senior, shared a basement apartment off-campus. Both had survived their stay at BYU thus far without joining the Church. I counted about sixty people in the congregation, including the eight in the choir. I was thrilled to be with them.

Pastor Don invited us over the next week for a barbecue and planning meeting. Don had come to faith in Christ as an adult. He loved his ministry in Provo and preached with zeal against the errors of Mormon doctrine. While we were waiting for others to arrive, Don showed me a page in the back of his Bible with a collection of verses that contradicted Mormon doctrine.

"Hey, let me see that! I'm on Mormon doctrine overload." I craned to have a look at his Bible. "I've got to ask you about some verses. How about that 'baptism for the dead'? And what about that 'preaching to the spirits in prison' verse?"

Don laughed. "You haven't heard the end of those verses. But don't worry. The Apostle Paul wasn't teaching us to baptize for the dead. He was pointing out that even pagans of that day believed in the resurrection. Their practice of baptizing for the dead demonstrates their belief in life after death. Paul never said 'we' baptize for the dead;

he said 'they' do. Christ Himself never mentioned it."

"As for 1 Peter 3, there are several possible explanations. Maybe Christ's spirit was upon Noah when he preached to the souls imprisoned by sin in the days of the flood. Maybe Christ did go and announce salvation to the faithful followers from the Old Testament era. It doesn't say Christ is still preaching to them. We don't know for sure, but you can't accept a whole doctrine built on that one puzzling verse. Mormons use all kinds of verses out of context to support their doctrines."

"Thanks, Don. Can I copy down this list?[4] "

I eagerly introduced myself to everyone I hadn't met. I recognized Diane Cross as the church pianist. She was trim and peppy and looked about thirty years old.

"What brings you to BYU?" I asked her.

Diane's merry laugh rang out. "What brings anybody here! Divine providence? Insanity? I'm teaching piano on campus. And I get to be the faculty sponsor for the BSU."

"Wow. That's cool."

I met Victor Hogstrom, an international student from Liberia, one of the rare Blacks at BYU. Victor was a senior, majoring in communications and international relations. Ironically, he—a Christian—was the producer of a religious news program on KBYU-TV. I wondered if he ever stood in *front* of the camera with that loud shirt and that big Afro hairdo.

Then I met Dawnena Walkingstick, a Cherokee Native American from North Carolina, new to BYU as a transfer student. Dawnena's straight black hair and angular features gave her an elegant look. I understood why her classy style when she told me she had traveled with "Up with People" for two years before going to college. I was pleased to learn that she lived in another building in Helaman Halls, my dormitory complex. We couldn't stop talking about our common experience thus far at the "Y."

I said, "By the way, did you know you are a Lamanite?"

Dawnena laughed. "Ha! A Lamanite! I've heard that about fifty times this week. You know that if I join the Church and obey the commandments, my skin will turn lighter? White skin is supposed to be a sign of holiness."

"Oh, brother." It was the sweet start of a lasting friendship.

After dinner, Don spoke. "As you know, John Cole agreed to be the president of the Baptist Student Union. This week he will submit our constitution and turn in some paperwork. Gary, Carol, and Diane, you need to sign those forms, too."

"We'd like to hold BSU meetings every week. How about Monday nights? After we're registered, we can meet on campus, but Victor, could we meet at your place this week?"

"Okay, but my place is small," said Victor.

On Monday night Dawnena and I went together to Victor's small basement room. We sat on Victor's bed, which practically filled his room. The only other pieces of furniture were a small desk and a television.

John and Gary showed up, and we made room for them on the bed. Victor put his studies aside and said, "Diane can't come tonight, so let's begin."

John handed me a form to sign. "Hey everybody, get this. No groups can meet on Monday nights because of Family Home Evening."

"Family Home Evening?" Dawnena and I said in unison.

"Right," said John. "Every Monday night, LDS families meet for a devotional lesson, prayer, an activity, and refreshments. It's an LDS family tradition."

"But we're not Mormon." Dawn said. "Last I checked."

"Oh, but every student is assigned to a 'family.' You are in a group, even if you're not LDS. They'll come find you. I hoped we might substitute BSU for Family Home Evening, but no such luck. Can we meet on Tuesday nights?"

"Sure."

John asked, "Does anyone know what a Baptist

Student Union is supposed to do? It seems like we ought to make some plans, but I've never been in a BSU before."

"Me either," I said. Neither had Victor or Gary or Dawnena.

John offered a suggestion. "Pastor Don said that a few years ago the students showed a filmstrip series called 'What Baptists Believe.' It was a good way to introduce ourselves to Mormons. We could do that sometime."

We sat around for a while, and finally Victor turned on the television. At 11 p.m., John adjourned the first BSU meeting.

On Friday, John called. "Gary and I are going to the drive-in movie tonight. Wanna come? We're inviting everyone. We'll pick you up at eight."

John, Victor, Dawnena and I squeezed into Gary's car with our pillows and blankets. We ate popcorn and even drank Coca-Cola, an illegal beverage on campus because of the caffeine. It wasn't an official BSU meeting, but it was great camaraderie.

Sunday mornings became a highlight of my week because of these friends. The families in the church also loved the BYU students and prayed for us. They sometimes invited us to Sunday dinner or brought us sacks of fresh fruit.

Our Tuesday night meetings took shape too. Diane

Cross regularly joined us on Tuesday nights, and we started studying the Bible during our meetings. Diane was a good sport and loved to laugh, so on Halloween night we decided to play a prank on her. She lived in an apartment, so we couldn't very well decorate her yard with toilet paper.

"What could we do to Diane's car?" John wondered.

"We could newspaper it," said Dawnena.

Late that night we sneaked out to Diane's parking lot with piles of newspapers and a hose. We soaked sheets of newspaper and plastered them all over her car. When the whole car was covered with newspaper, we soaked it again so it would stay wet until morning. I laughed myself to sleep that night and could hardly wait for Diane's reaction.

I called Dawnena the next day. "Have you heard from Diane?"

"Nope. The guys haven't either."

We all waited several days. We were sure she knew who did it, but we began to wonder whether the whole prank had blown away during the night. When we saw Diane on Sunday, she still didn't mention anything about her car.

Finally, weeks later, John asked her about it. She laughed and said, "It was so hard to keep from telling you, but that next morning, I couldn't find my car! I looked and looked and finally recognized it by the shape. I couldn't stop laughing. Of course I knew who did it."

I had to ask, "Did it all come off okay?"

"Yeah, but it was frozen! Where were you guys when I needed someone to clean it off?"

What a difference a few weeks had made. I was no longer alone; I had found my little island in the vast ocean of Mormonism.

chapter four

*A*s for academics, I liked my music classes. I liked my horn teacher. I liked playing in the Symphonic Wind Ensemble. And I liked my American History class, where the professor lectured for three hours straight without using a single book or note. I took notes till my fingers cramped. But I liked it. I liked my class in Spanish grammar and composition, conducted all in Spanish.

I didn't like my religion class. Freshmen were supposed to take Book of Mormon first. The BYU religion requirements were stiff; every student had to complete fourteen semester credits in religion before graduation. I didn't want to study the Book of Mormon, but I knew something about the New Testament, so I had registered for a New Testament class.

My religion class troubles had started on the first day when I couldn't find the building in an unfamiliar part of campus. I walked in just in time to take the last empty seat, front row center, practically on top of tall, hawk-eyed

Professor Pratt as he began his introductory lecture.

"I assume you have all completed Religion 121 and 122, Book of Mormon. We will refer to material from that course as well as your knowledge of the Church. Some of you more recent converts to the church have less background; I understand that, but I expect you to participate intelligently in our class discussions. Your grade depends on class participation.

"Bring your New Testament to class. I will use the Greek New Testament. By the way, I also teach Greek 101. I earned my Ph.D. in Ancient Languages."

A Ph.D. in Ancient Languages? Greek 101? Did I, a Gentile freshman, belong in this class? Should I drop it and go sign up for Book of Mormon? That's where freshmen belonged. How was I ever going to make it through the semester? After two days of agonized waffling, I decided to stay in the New Testament class, study hard, and hide in the back row, though there wasn't much room to hide in a class with fewer than thirty students and all this participation again. I liked getting good grades; I wished I could just sit and listen like in history class.

We began studying the Book of Matthew right away. The LDS theology was extraordinary even before we left the first chapter. Dr. Pratt said that Jesus had received His spiritual life ages before as the result of a union between Heavenly Father and Heavenly Mother. In the same way, he said, all of us are "spirit children" of Heavenly Father and Heavenly Mother, so Jesus is our spiritual brother. Regarding the "divine conception" (the LDS term for the virgin birth) he said, "Jesus received a body on earth when Heavenly Father came bodily to earth and had relations with Mary.[5]

I was aghast at this comment. The very passage we were studying, Matthew 1:18 said, "she was found to be with child through the Holy Spirit." But who was I to speak up against a Ph.D. in a room full of Mormon students? My heart was pounding, but I didn't know what to say. I looked around to see what other students thought.

One asked, "What do Protestants believe about the divine conception?"

With a smile, Dr. Pratt said, "The Protestants believe Jesus was conceived by relations between Mary and Joseph the carpenter."

I was shocked. I couldn't just sit there and say nothing, but I was afraid I'd cry if I raised my hand. After class I gripped my books and walked to the front.

"Brother Pratt," I said in a controlled tone, "I don't think what you said about the Protestants' belief is true."

"About Jesus' conception? Several converts from Protestantism have told me they were taught that Jesus was born of Joseph and Mary. Of course, I can't speak for all Protestants."

He didn't ask why I disagreed with him. Having used up my meager courage, I fled. At least I'd said something. I was glad I didn't cry.

That evening I called Dawnena and told her I hated my religion class.

She said, "Let's go get a Dr Pepper." Dr Pepper, her favorite beverage, was laced with caffeine so we went off campus. Dawn listened to my woes, and she prayed for me. Dawnena was taking Book of Mormon, which she described as LDS catechism. But it didn't seem as scary as mine, and at least there was one other Gentile in her class.

In another lecture, Dr. Pratt was teaching about the conflict between Satan and the Church, and he mentioned the great and abominable church. Always nervous and defensive, I tried to figure out what he meant by that.

Someone proposed, "I think there is more to the great and abominable church than just Catholics—anything outside the LDS Church is of Satan." Several other students nodded agreement.

So maybe they meant Catholicism. In a rush of courage, I raised my hand.

"How would you define the great and abominable church?" I asked.

"Go read 1 Nephi again, oh you of short memories. It's the apostasy. It's the church of the devil. There are only two churches, remember? The church of the lamb of God and the church of the devil. Chapter fourteen."

I trusted our textbook, the New Testament (though we often referred to Joseph Smith's Inspired Version of the Bible), but I was wary of other sources like the Book of Mormon (where 1 Nephi was found) or other Latter-day Scriptures. On the other hand, some verses from LDS sources sounded "true"—especially ones that mirrored Bible passages. Besides, if I rejected what every LDS professor said, I'd have to discard music, history, language, and science. Couldn't I trust what I learned about those subjects? Could I believe even some of what I learned in religion class? Simply rejecting everything people said was just as brainless as accepting everything.

On Tuesdays and Thursdays, I often woke up with a headache in dread of religion class. I didn't make any friends in there; they were all older than I was, and they felt like spiritual strangers. I showed up and sat through every class with grim determination, but I kept the long countdown to the end of the semester. I wrote my term paper on a non-controversial topic: "Peter in the Gospel of Mark."

John and Gary had warned us about Family Home Evening on Monday nights, and sure enough, Janet and I were assigned to a "family." I caved in to peer pressure and found myself sitting in a Family Home Evening meeting.

The group consisted of neighbors from our hall. We had counterparts in the boys' dorm, but we only met with them on special occasions. After introductions and snacks we chose a topic for study on Monday nights. The group voted for the Pearl of Great Price, one of the Latter-day Scriptures.

As the meeting adjourned, I hung back to talk with a short Asian girl named Liz Sze, who said she was from Hong Kong. "Are you Mormon?" I whispered.

"No."

"Are you any religion?"

"I'm an atheist."

"You are an atheist? I'm a Baptist."

"My grandfather was a Baptist preacher in Hong Kong."

I decided that my mission in Family Home Evening was to look out for Liz, so I attended every week. Everyone (except Liz, who refused) took turns leading the discussion. Eventually it was my turn. I read aloud from the 5th Chapter of Moses, the first book in the Pearl of Great Price:

"9. And in that day the Holy Ghost fell upon Adam, which beareth record of the Father and the Son, saying: I am the Only Begotten of the Father from the beginning, henceforth and forever, that as thou hast fallen thou mayest be redeemed, and all mankind, even as many as will. 10. And in that day Adam blessed God and was filled, and began to prophesy concerning all the families of the earth, saying: Blessed be the name of God, for because of my transgression my eyes are opened, and in this life I shall have joy, and again in the flesh I shall see God."

The words seemed to stick in my mouth. They sounded like King James' English, but to me they didn't sound like God's Word. I sat and watched Liz stare at the fish poster on my wall. I was sure she wasn't listening. Why did she even come to these meetings? My thoughts were interrupted by the discussion.

"Look at Moses 5:11," said Cindy, who lived across the hall. She read, "And Eve, his wife, heard all these things and was glad, saying: Were it not for our transgression we never should have had seed, and never should have known good and evil, and the joy of our redemption, and the eternal life which God giveth unto all the obedient.' You see, because of Adam's transgression, we can receive eternal life through obedience. Adam helped us by eating the fruit."

Everyone agreed.

I said, "Did you say Adam and Eve's sin helped us?"

Janet answered, "Adam was actually obeying the higher, ultimate plan of God. We know that you only believe the Bible, Carol, but the modern Scriptures such as this one fill in the gaps the Bible leaves." She straightened her blouse.

I dropped out of the conversation again, angry and

hurt. I got a knot in my stomach whenever I discussed doctrine, and so far I hadn't changed anyone's mind. Certainly not Janet's. I was compliant by nature, but eventually even I could recognize a losing battle.

I saw Liz the next day. "I might stop going to Family Home Evening," I said. "Why do you keep going?"

Liz shrugged. "Since I don't go to church."

I didn't understand her logic. "Do you want to go to our church?"

"I used to go in Hong Kong a lot. Yeah, I'll go."

Liz came to our church and to the Baptist Student Union, and we both disappeared from Family Home Evening. At first, when I made excuses for my absence, Janet arranged meeting times to fit my schedule. Finally I told her, "Don't expect me to come anymore."

"Carol, I'm disappointed. We love having you."

"I know you want to include me. Thanks, but it's just not my cup of tea."

Now it was tense in the dorm on Mondays. Janet prepared her Family Home Evening lessons flamboyantly every Monday afternoon. I tried to avoid my neighbors on Mondays. I couldn't very well stay in my room and study. I spent Monday evenings in my practice room or in the library.

I decided to hunt for other Gentile students. I asked the resident assistant on our floor if she knew any non-members.

"Well there's Peggy... I think she's some sort of Protestant. And you probably know Tammy, the Lutheran girl."

I went straightaway to knock on Peggy's door. The girl who answered the door was plain and chubby.

"Hi, I'm Carol," I said. "Are you Peggy?"

"Yes." She looked warily at me.

"I live down the hall and I'm not LDS. I heard that you aren't either. I wanted to meet you."

"I was baptized last week."

"You were?"

"Wanna come in?"

The walls of her room were covered with posters of the Osmond family. "I owe a lot to them," she said, motioning to one poster. "It was because of the Osmonds that I found the Church. Back home I listened to all their albums and read all about them, and I knew that they were Mormons, so I decided to come to BYU. Did you know the Osmonds have a home in Provo? I saw Donny one day.

"Being here has really straightened me out. Before this I was into drugs and everything. Now I have discovered the truth of the Church. If you haven't yet, don't worry. Pray, and you will feel a burning in your bosom about the truth of these things. I'll pray for you, too."

"Thanks." After that, I needed to rest up before going to find Tammy. I went back to my room, where Janet was deep in conversation with Barbara from our Family Home Evening group. Barbara was another new convert to Mormonism and was often bewildered about the doctrines of the Church.

"I can't believe there is a god before our God, and another God before Him, and that we will become gods too," she said.

"Yes, Barbara, these things are hard to understand," said Janet. "When I first heard the story of Noah's Ark, I laughed. But after a while, I believed it. It comes with time and faith. Just be patient." Janet looked up. "Oh, hi Carol!"

"Sorry to interrupt."

"No problem." Janet closed her Scriptures. "We've got to stop talking and start studying anyway." Barbara left, and I sat down and opened my history book.

"Oh, Carol, your visiting teachers came by. I told them to come again later."

"My visiting teachers?"

"Yes. The branch assigns us each two visiting teachers, just like at home. They bring a spiritual lesson and see how you are doing every month."

"I'm not in the branch."

"You are on the roll. You just aren't active. We also have two home teachers that come once a month. They are our spiritual guides. Speaking of which, one of ours is really handsome." Her voice went up at the end of that sentence, as though she were tossing it at me.

"What happens if I don't want all these teachers?"

"I don't know. I always want them."

I plopped down on my bed. "Do you know someone named Tammy on our hall?"

"Oh yes. I see her in Sacrament Meeting. She's in
Room 2210."

"Is she LDS?"

"No."

I closed my book and went for a walk outside, hugging my sweater around myself against the chill I was feeling. I stopped by Dawnena's room, but she wasn't there. I
knew if she had been there, she would have walked with
me. I walked back and knocked on Tammy's door just to
get it over with.

I recognized her from the community bathroom.

"Hi, Tammy, I'm Carol."

"Oh you're the non-LDS from down the hall. You
don't go to the branch, do you? I'm training to be a visiting
teacher right now."

"You're training to be a visiting teacher?" I felt that
news in my stomach.

"Why don't you come to the branch? How else can
you get to know people? You don't have to be LDS to come."

"I go to the Baptist church on Sundays. I don't want
to be in the branch."

"Oh, but you miss out on so much. That's where all the social life is. I met Peter in our branch. Do you know him? His father is a General Authority. When I turn eighteen, his dad is coming down from Salt Lake City to baptize me."

"Why do you have to wait till you're eighteen?"

Tammy looked down. "My parents are devoted Lutherans. They don't understand. I saved up my own money to come here."

I kept the visit brief. "Tammy, if you ever want to talk with someone outside the Church, come see me. I'm down in 2204."

She never did.

A couple of weeks later Don Plott showed me a computer printout labeled "Baptist by Denomination." He said, "I just got this from the University. Would you be interested in contacting some of these students?"

I looked over the list of about 25 names. "I'm not even on here," I said. "I probably didn't put down that I was a Baptist. I never called myself that till I came here." I gave it back to Pastor Don. "Too bad we didn't have this when school started, before they all got converted to Mormonism!"

"I'm pleased that the school gave us this at all; we didn't even request it."

John and I divided the names, and Dawnena and I

went looking for the girls. Of those we contacted, a couple were already or soon-to-be Latter-day Saints. A couple of others didn't want to be identified as Baptists. We didn't make any new friends.

I did cross paths with Linda, my old buddy from the freshman seminar. "Hey Carol! Great to see you! How ya' doin'?"

"Fine."

"Everything is going great for me—coming here was the best decision I ever made! I'm engaged! And I'm going to be baptized this Saturday. Can you come?"

"I really can't come. I'm sorry. But good luck."

I experienced my first General Conference in October. This Church-wide devotional conference is held twice a year in October and April, and the whole LDS world stops and listens. Classes were dismissed on Friday so students could hear the Apostles' and other General Authorities' speeches broadcast live over KSL television and radio. On my way down the hall on Saturday I heard the message droning in unison from several dorm rooms.

I could hardly ask Janet to turn her radio off; she was hoping I'd stop and listen to some truth myself. I went outside and saw groups of students relaxed on blankets, doing homework while listening to their radios. In the cafeteria, the talks were broadcast over the sound system. I finally took refuge in the library.

After President Kimball's closing address on Sunday, the radios were turned off, but a new vigor pulsed through the LDS community. The next night when Janet returned from Family Home Evening, she said, "Oh Carol, by the way, I invited some visitors—the missionaries from our stake. They'll be downstairs to meet us in a few minutes."

"Missionaries? Janet! You should have asked me first."

"I didn't want you to say no. They *are* really nice." Janet gripped her Scriptures with fervor.

"I don't want to talk to the missionaries."

"Carol, please. It's too late to call them back."

Janet escorted me down to the lobby where two eager spiffy fellows stepped forward and shook my hand. "You must be Carol. I am Elder Davis and this is Elder Perry. We serve as part-time missionaries in your stake. We're students too, but we've both served two-year missions. We'd like to invite you to join us for some home study lessons for investigators of the Church."

"I'm not an investigator."

"We understand," said Elder Davis too quickly. "The purpose of the lessons is simply to inform you about the Church history and its beliefs. We know you're Baptist."

I stole a glance at Janet, who looked as though she'd been caught taking a noble idea too far.

The elder continued. "These discussions simply help you understand us better. We feel it is important to keep an open mind before making judgments. When would you like to begin?"

I needed time to think, but I didn't want to seem weak. I took evasive action by saying, "I'd like to wait."

"Fine. How about a week from Sunday?" These guys were fast talkers, and persistent, too.

"I guess so." I was good at saying yes, but no didn't come as easily.

Firm handshakes occurred again, and then the elders were gone. I thought Janet's face was going to get a cramp from smiling. She squeezed my arm and said, "Carol, I'm so happy for you! I care about you so much."

"I know you do. Thanks." I had asked God to make me brave, and here was my chance to show courage. But I didn't sleep well. I told Sheryl the next day in class. Naturally, she thought the lessons were a great idea.

When I asked Dawnena what she thought, she said, "I don't know much about the discussions, but don't ask *me* to take them with you."

On Sunday, Pastor Don said, "The word 'discussions' doesn't really describe those lessons. The missionaries ask you leading questions, and you answer them. They tell you something and then get you to agree to it."

The more I thought about it, the less I wanted to go through with these lessons. I had mentioned this situation in a letter home, and I quickly received a response from my father.

> "Dear Carol,
>
> ...I am concerned about you getting involved in the Mormon teaching program. Matthew 7:15 says, 'Beware of false prophets, which come to you in sheep's clothing, but inwardly they are ravening wolves.' Honey, the chance that you will gain any ground in that situation is extremely remote.
>
> Don't feel defeated if you choose to back out in the middle of the program. I must alert you to the spiritual dangers involved. Your mother and I will keep you constantly in our prayers. Let the Lord be your guide...
>
> Love,
> Dad

This was the first letter I ever remember receiving from Dad. Mom was the letter writer in our family. And the only other time I'd seen Dad this forceful was the day I came home from junior high music camp with green eye shadow caked around my eyes.

I looked at Dad's letter for a while, then I called Elder Davis and said, "I have decided not to take the discussions right now."

There was a long silence. The elder said, "Why?"

"Several people, including my father, have counseled me against it. I'm going to wait."

"Wait for what? Are you afraid?"

"Maybe."

"Carol, I challenge you to discover for yourself the truth of the Church. I promise that you will gain a testimony of the truth of our Church when you participate in these discussions. What we have to say is very significant and must be considered."

"I'm sorry. I hope you are not offended." With my dad to back me up, I had just enough strength to stick to my decision.

"Have you read the Book of Mormon?"

"I have looked it over. I'm taking New Testament right now."

"Carol, you know the Bible is incomplete. The Book of Mormon fills in the gaps the Bible leaves. I challenge you to read it and ask God if these things are true. If you ask with sincere faith and real intent, He will manifest the truth to you."

When I finally hung up, I couldn't hold back the tears. Janet came over and said, "Sounds like that guy was hard on you."

"Maybe I'm just too sensitive."

"Give me his phone number. I'm going to tell him off." She marched out of the room, thin-lipped, to use the phone in the lobby.

Soon she returned and said, "Well, I told *him*. He didn't mean to be rude, but he said to tell you he was sorry. I'm sorry too, Carol. I just want to help you find the truth."

"I know. But it's hard to have my faith under attack all the time."

Each November the Utah-Idaho Southern Baptist association sponsored a retreat for students. This fall, the retreat was at Idaho State University in Pocatello. Don Plott and Diane joined Dawnena, Victor, Gary, John, Liz, and me for the trip to Idaho.

The registrar said in amazement, "You're from Brigham Young University? There's a BSU at Brigham Young University?" As the word spread, we became the heroes of the weekend. After the months of spiritual isolation we were overjoyed to meet Christian students from other universities. They rallied around us and promised to pray for us. We caught a vision of what a BSU ministry could be from the other students. We even volunteered to host the coming spring retreat in Provo.

At the closing session, one student from each university shared what God was doing at that school. Pastor Don asked Liz Sze to represent us.

Liz walked to the podium and said, "I have seen Christ's love in the BSU at Brigham Young University. I can't understand why these people care so much about me. I won't even accept Christ into my life, but these friends keep on praying for me. Even though I'm not a Christian, they never give up on me." Liz paused as though deciding whether to say more, and then walked slowly back to her seat. Don stood and led the audience in prayer for Liz.

Later I said, "Liz, you don't seem like an atheist."

"I know. I do believe in God, but I'm not going to be converted. Before I came here, my friends said, 'Ha, ha, Liz, you're going to get religion at that Mormon school.' Well, I'm not going to get Mormonism or any other religion." I empathized with her and determined to love her without pressure.

Maybe it started on that trip, or maybe before, but we who spent so much time together developed a bad habit. It started with little jokes about being Gentiles. Then someone started making cracks about Sainthood and our friends who called themselves "gods in embryo."

Then it got more personal when Gary said, "Hey, have you heard about the bulletproof underwear yet?"

"No."

"Aren't you taking P.E.?"

"I am," said Dawnena.

"Well, next time you're in the locker room, look around. Mormons who are married or have been on missions wear secret underwear to keep them safe."

"No way," I said. "I don't believe it."

Dawnena, her face wrinkled, said, "Come to think of it, I have seen a couple people in my gym class wear another layer under their regular stuff, but they take it off for P.E."

"That's it," Gary said. "That's the bulletproof underwear. I told you.[6]"

I was a little embarrassed, but very curious. I decided to sign up for P.E. next semester.

This kind of cynicism afforded us some stress relief, but it never left us feeling good about ourselves. But now with only two weeks until finals, everyone disappeared into studies. There was little time for fellowship or missionary activity fomr anyone.

I was eager to go home for Christmas. I walked downtown to a travel agent and made a plane reservation for Friday afternoon, after my last scheduled exam.

The first week of December, Brother Turner offered to give that Friday final early; he didn't want to be the one to keep us at school any longer than necessary. Now my last exam was history on Thursday morning. I walked down to the travel agent and rescheduled my flight for Thursday afternoon.

Then the history professor took a vote: Did the students want to take their final early? Overwhelmingly, yes they did. Now I was free after my Wednesday morning exam. I walked back down to the travel agent. She changed it, but sternly said to me, "This is the last time I am changing your reservation."

In January, my grades came in the mail. I got a B in American History; I'd never worked so hard for a B before. But I had an A in religion! Late in the semester, I had finally told Dr. Pratt that I was a Christian. However, I wished I'd stood up more for my faith. At least after braving one semester, I was still a Gentile.

chapter five

I arrived back in Provo on a cold, dark January night. I braced myself against the icy wind as I stepped out of the airport shuttle in front of the dormitory. Heaving open the dormitory door, I dragged my suitcase up the stairs.

I dialed Dawnena's number. Her telephone rang unanswered. I called John. No answer there. Gary had graduated in December. Feeling uneasy, I called Diane Cross. I was relieved when she answered.

"Hi Carol, welcome back!" She was her usual chipper self.

"Where is everybody?"

"Victor's here, but I haven't heard from anyone else yet."

My door opened and in staggered Janet under a load of luggage. I greeted her with a hug. "Hi roomie, it's good to see you!" BYU was still strange to me, but less frightening than before.

Classes started, and we still hadn't heard from John or Dawnena. Finally, John called. I shouted into the phone,

"Where have you been?"

"I'm in Provo right now, but I'm not staying for the semester. I don't have the money for tuition. I can finish school at home for less than half the cost. I came to pack up."

"But John, you're our BSU president!" I felt panicky.

"I know. I'm sorry, Carol."

I felt my support system crumbling beneath me. Gary was gone, and now John was leaving. And where was Dawnena?

Then Diane called. "I just talked with Dawnena. Her grandfather passed away. She stayed in North Carolina to help her family. She should be here by the late registration deadline next Wednesday."

"She better be. I don't know if I can survive without her."

"Carol, that sounds so dramatic!"

I wasn't being dramatic—I really thought I'd perish without my friend Dawn.

Victor and I met at Diane's apartment. I stared out her window at the snowy town. "We're it, I guess," I said.

"Yes, Miss Carol, you are now the president," Victor declared smugly.

"I don't think so. I'm the secretary-treasurer. Victor, I think *you* should be the president."

"Oh no. Not me. My course load is too heavy. As it is I'm not going to graduate on time."

I got a sinking feeling. As loyal as a Girl Scout, I knew I couldn't let my friends down. I would answer the call of duty. But I was afraid of the responsibility and even of the title "president."

Diane said, "Carol, you'll be a great president. I'll help you. I'm sure Dawnena will be back, and she'll help. Come on; let's make some plans. We talked about showing that film series, 'What Baptists Believe.' I still think that's a good idea.

"Carol, have you seen them? Each film covers a topic like God, Christ, the church, and salvation. We could show a couple at a time, and have a discussion afterwards. To publicize, we could put up posters and advertise in the newspaper. Hey Victor, wouldn't this be a news item for your KBYU show, *Religion Today*?"

"Yes, in fact I'm always looking for guests to interview. Carol, you'd be perfect."

"Oh, *great*. Now you want me to be on TV."

"Carol, we need the publicity. You'll be famous!" Diane laughed and jostled my slumping shoulder. "Now let's get this on the calendar, the sooner the better. How about we start on January 21? Hey Carol, when you go reserve a room, check on the weekend of March 28 and 29, too; that's when we're hosting the BSU convention."

"In the Wilkinson Student Center? Do you think they'll let a bunch of Baptists meet right on campus?"

"We'll never know if you don't ask."

"Okay. I'll try." I shrugged.

The next day I ventured into the scheduling office. The secretary froze when I introduced myself as the president of the Baptist Student Union, but she wrote down the film series on the university calendar and assigned us a room in the Wilkinson Center. I tried to act casual as I requested a room for the BSU convention in March. This time she stood up and walked into the back office. When she returned, she said, "The director approved your request."

The night before late registration ended, Dawnena called. "Hey Carol, I'm back!"

"Thank God! I'm coming over. I can't wait to see you."

I grabbed Liz and hurried over to Dawn's dorm room. Diane was already there. "Trying to scare us, huh?" Diane said.

"Yeah, sorry about that." Dawn smiled. "I scared myself, too. But I am glad to be back."

Dawn and I were at Victor's house later that week when Amos, a Nigerian friend of his, dropped by. I loved Amos' accent; he rolled his r's and rounded his o's in a curious brogue. But his words were bitter and angry. Dawn and I walked back toward campus with Amos, and I asked him what he found hardest about being at BYU.

He glared at me, jaw tight. "You don't know what it's like to be hated for the color of your skin. People here won't even make my acquaintance. Only once in two years have I been friendly to a girl and she refused to be seen with me. I vowed never to befriend a Mormon girl again. You are the first non-Mormon girls I have met."

I pitied him. "Amos, believe me," I said, "our whole country's not like this."

"I dream about a transfer to another school, but I'm here on scholarship." Amos stopped and said, "Here's my house. I live here with three of my countrymen. Carol, before you go, may I ask a favor? I'd like to talk with you again. Will you give me your phone number?"

How could I say no? I didn't want to be like those other girls that rejected Amos. I wrote my number for him on a scrap of paper.

As we crossed the street, Dawn elbowed me and said, "Wonder why he asked you and not me?"

"Maybe I'm prettier."

"I don't think so."

"Maybe he could tell I'm not good at saying no."

"Yeah, that's probably it."

"I'm afraid of all that anger. I hope he doesn't call."

"He probably will."

When I told Janet about Amos, she said. "I think he's exaggerating. I always try to be polite to everyone. And the Church isn't prejudiced about skin color. But I'll tell you the teaching about Blacks. Negroes are descendants of Cain, and anyone with Negro blood carries the curse of Cain. We know from latter-day revelation that the curse of Cain was dark skin and Negroid features. No person of Negro lineage may hold the priesthood or enter the temples. Of course they may join the Church, and many have."

"I wonder why they would join a Church that believes they are cursed."

"Carol, our Heavenly Father loves Blacks, but because of the curse, He has placed some limitations on them. We believe that in the future, as man evolves, Blacks will overcome the limitations of the curse and become eligible to hold the priesthood.[7]

On Saturday afternoon Victor called me. "I just talked with Amos," he said. "He was injured today, and he invited you to his house. His roommates are fixing supper."

"What happened to him?"

"Come find out. I told him we would come together."

When Victor and I arrived, Amos's roommates greeted us. "Come in; we've been expecting you."

My hands felt clammy, and I tucked them under

my arms. The men escorted me into Amos's room where he was propped up with pillows, holding an icebag to his face. When he adjusted the bag I saw his swollen jaw and black eye.

Amos motioned to a chair beside the bed. I sat on the edge and said, "Amos, what happened?"

I strained to understand his pronunciation. "A fellow from Tonga came and beat me up. Those Polynesians think they're better than we Africans are just because they're Mormons. He lives next door and doesn't own a stove, so he came to use ours. He put a pot on the stove and left. I was using the stove too, you see, so I moved his pot to the back burner. He walked back in and struck me in the face. He said nothing. That's all I remember until policemen were here. I was taken to the infirmary for X-rays."

"Is anything broken?"

"No, just bruised."

Amos's roommates were standing around. One said, "Victor, it's a quarter till seven. Are you ready to leave?"

I looked up at Victor. "Are we going already? I thought we were staying for supper."

"You are, Carol. Eddie and I are going to a meeting. I'll be back in time to take you home."

I glared at Victor, then looked around at the friendly Nigerians and turned back to Amos.

"Who is this guy from Tonga? He's LDS?"

Amos said, "There are lots of Mormons in Tonga. Forty percent of their population is Mormon. That fellow is in our branch. I see him almost every Sunday."

"You see him at church? You go to meetings?"

"Of course. We're all members except Eddie. He's Seventh-Day Adventist."

"You're a member of the LDS Church?" I was astounded. "I thought you hated the Mormon Church!"

"I do. We were all baptized to save tuition costs. I don't believe any of it, but I did give a talk in Sacrament Meeting about prejudice one time."

There was a knock at the door, and George left to answer it. In came two blond guests. The silence was awkward until one said, "Amos, we heard about your accident. We're sorry. We came to see how you are."

Amos was silent.

One guest said to me, "I'm Richard and this is Jacob. We're his home teachers. How is Amos?"

"I'm fine." Amos spoke.

I struck up a little conversation with the fellows, returned missionaries who lived in a house around the corner. I felt sorry for them. They were trying their best to be friendly, but there was something stiff about their compassion. No wonder. They must have been even more uncomfortable than I was. One of them looked at his watch two or three times. No one else spoke, and finally the largest African roommate ushered the home teachers to the door.

George poked his head in from the kitchen. "Dinner's ready."

I sat down to a Nigerian meal of stew and soft dough. I watched the experts tear off a glob of dough, roll it into a ball, and use the ball to scoop up a bite of strange stew. There was no silverware. I never did get the hang of eating it, but I wasn't hungry anyway.

"The only reason Richard came to see you, Amos, is because he had to. He doesn't really care about you. He's a hypocrite," said George.

I rose to the defense of the home teachers. "Amos, you hardly gave them a chance to care about you. You were rude."

Amos lashed out. "These people act superior to us. They ignore us or else they are so arrogant it makes me ill."

The large man spoke. "I knew it would be like this before I came. I knew I would experience hatred."

I listened to the men tell their stories, wanting to believe they were exaggerating, as Janet supposed. Their attitudes definitely needed work, but I felt sure they weren't making up the stories. Finally Victor and Eddie returned.

"Carol, are you ready to go?"

"Yes."

I gave my regards to Amos and his roommates.

George said, "Thank you for having the courage to come to our house."

Amos never did ask me out on a date, but after that night I went out of my way to be friendly to African students.

At a BSU meeting before the "What Baptists Believe" film series we previewed the first two filmstrips and we designed posters to advertise the series. The next day Liz took them to the organizations office for approval and posted them on bulletin boards around campus.

On Friday morning I rose early, spent a long time in front of the mirror and reported to the KBYU-TV studio for the taping of *Religion Today*. The host, David Peterson, met me in the lobby and questioned me about the BSU so he'd know what to say on the air.

Soon Victor appeared in the doorway. "Five minutes, Dave. Hi, Carol. My, don't you look lovely! Are you ready for your television debut?"

"Yes, Victor." Victor was too much of a tease. David and I walked on the set, and I took a deep breath to quiet my nerves. I felt my cheeks turning red from the heat of the floodlights as we sat still waiting for our cue.

Victor called out to me from the darkness, "No scratching yourself, Carol. Keep your hands in your lap." I gave him a friendly scowl.

During the interview, David asked me what a Baptist Student Union was and what it did. He asked about our film series. He emphasized that I was a freshman and the president of the BSU. The five minutes passed quickly, and I was relieved when David said, "Thank you, Carol, for being part of our program today." We sat motionless until the camera shifted to the news desk. David tiptoed off the set and motioned for me to follow. As I left the studio, he said, "Good job, Carol. Be sure to watch the broadcast tomorrow at 6 p.m."

The next evening I went to the TV room in our dorm. As their show ended, I asked the girls watching if I could switch to *Religion Today*. When I appeared on the screen, one girl exclaimed, "That's you? You're the president of the Baptist Student Union?"

I nodded and we all kept watching. At the end of the interview, someone said, "I didn't even know there were any Baptists at BYU. I can't believe they even allow a Baptist Student Union."

"We're a campus club like any other club. The administration doesn't seem to mind. Maybe they allow it because it makes the school look diverse."

This same girl said loudly, "I'm sure I won't make it to your film series, so why don't you tell us what Baptists believe?"

Having previewed the films, I could say, "We believe the Bible. It is our only authority on doctrine. We believe God has preserved His Word down through the centuries."

"We believe the Bible to be the Word of God as far as it is correctly translated," she parroted from the LDS Articles of Faith.

"Yes, I know," I said. I continued, "We also believe that man is by nature sinful and separated from God and can only be saved through faith in Jesus Christ."

"We believe that man shall become like God by perfect obedience to the commandments."

"Yes, I know." I could see that this conversation would only deteriorate. "Gotta go now. Thanks for letting me change the channel."

Janet, back from class, was curled up on her bed with a large scrapbook when I came in. She looked up. "Hi! How was the show?"

"Some girls in the TV room had opinions about it."

"Want me to go talk to them?"

"No thanks, Janet," I said. "Hey, what's that you're looking at? Is that a photo album?"

"This is my Book of Remembrance. Here, I'll show you." She made room for me to sit beside her. "This first part is my genealogy. You know the Church counsels us to trace our family history. Because my family has been in the Church for generations, most of our genealogy has been done. I copy it in my book and try to expand on it."

"Why does everybody do genealogy?"

"Many of our ancestors didn't have the chance to hear the gospel and be baptized, especially those before the restoration of the Church. So when we find those people's names, we baptize them by proxy. In fact, I'm going to the Provo Temple next week to do baptisms."

"You are? Baptisms for the dead?"

"Yes, I'll be a proxy. Church members around the world send in names of their ancestors, and the temple worker baptizes me in those names. These baptisms for the dead have to be done in temples, and not every place in the world has a temple yet. I've done it before. I'll probably be baptized about forty times. Usually young people are the proxies. I look forward to serving the Lord in this way."

"Wow. What else is in your book?" So far this was fascinating.

"My patriarchal blessing." She flipped past it. "I can't show it to you because it's sacred. Do you know what a patriarchal blessing is?"

"No."

"Every Saint has the privilege of receiving a blessing from a patriarch, a leader in the Church. The blessing tells us about our character, our future, what our special flower is, and things like that. I have a record here of everything he said."

"What's a patriarch?"

"Most every stake has a patriarch, a distinguished older man who has many years of leadership service in the Church."

"How does a patriarch know what to tell you?"

"He receives a revelation from the Lord. The patriarch is wise and discerns the mind of the Lord. Carol, the Church has so many blessings for us. I hope you can receive them."

"Thanks, Janet. Thanks for sharing your special book with me." I went down the hall to ask Liz about the posters for the film series.

"Yes, I put them up."

The next day I looked for our handiwork on the bulletin boards but found only one poster. Puzzled, I called her back.

Liz said, "I looked too. They're gone."

I got right on the phone. "Diane, someone took down our posters! Can you believe it?"

"It's okay, Carol. We still have that ad in the paper. Let's trust God, not our publicity."

On January 21 we met in the Wilkinson Center for the first episode of "What Baptists Believe." Ben Rivera, a deacon from our church and a wise and successful businessman, came to help answer questions. I welcomed the guests heartily as they arrived. By 7:30 about fifteen people had shown up.

We began the film, "What Baptists Believe about God," and then showed "What Baptists Believe about Salvation." Then we took the anticipated questions about the Trinity, salvation by grace, and heaven. Ben was calm and cheerful, and the discussion stayed cordial until we adjourned for cookies and punch.

Suddenly I heard a loud voice say "No! That's not right! You're twisting that verse!" An irate bald man was shouting and waving his Bible in Ben's face.

Ben stepped back and said gently, "It says, 'No man hath seen God at any time.' There's nothing to twist."

"Then it's a mistranslation! It can't be true because man *has* seen God. He came to earth and appeared bodily to Joseph Smith."

"The Bible teaches that God is a Spirit," Ben said. "For instance, John 4:24."

The man snapped three pages over in his Bible and read, "God is a Spirit and they that worship him must worship him in spirit and in truth" (KJV).

He slammed the Bible shut and said, "There's no point in carrying this any further."

As the man reached for his coat, Ben said, "I'll pray for you."

The man turned quickly and said, "You don't need to do that."

"I know, but I would like to."

"I prefer that you don't. My truth is so superior to your prayers that your prayers won't matter anyway. So don't pray for me!"

When the door closed behind him, Diane, Ben, and I exchanged wide-eyed looks. "What was his problem?" Diane wondered. "I think he was afraid of prayers."

"I am going to pray for him," said Ben. "And I'll pray that I'll be able to handle problems like that with grace."

Diane said, "Ben, you handled that with true grace. The problem is, the Bible doesn't say what Mormons want it to say. I'm sure it's frustrating for them to talk to us because the Bible simply doesn't back them up on certain points of doctrine."

The audience was smaller on the next three Tuesdays, and the angry man didn't come back. At the final session, Ben, a member of the Gideons, distributed Bibles. At our next meeting, Dawnena wondered, "Did this 'What Baptists Believe' effort do any good?"

"Not many people even came," I pointed out, as if no one else had noticed.

"But it was great publicity," said Victor.

"Yeah, it got me on your show," I said to him.

"I think it was worthwhile," Diane said. "Hundreds of people know about us now. You might even say we've put the BSU on the map."

chapter six

"*B*zzzzzz!"

    I stared at my alarm clock and sank back on the pillow. It was 3:30 a.m. My suitcase and French horn waited beside my bed. I had to report for bus check at 4:30 for the Wind Ensemble tour. I lurched out of bed, stumbled down to the bathroom, and splashed cold water on my face.

    When I returned to the room, the light was on and a pastry and jar of juice were arranged on a napkin on my desk. "Good morning!" Janet said cheerfully. "I didn't want you to go hungry. I also arranged for the flute player upstairs to walk to the bus with you because the sun won't be up yet. She'll be here at 4:15."

    "Janet, you're so nice to me!" Sometimes she drove me crazy, but she sure was helpful and kind. I hugged her and said, "Go back to sleep. I'll see you on Saturday."

    Sheryl wasn't in the Wind Ensemble; she played horn in the BYU Philharmonic Orchestra. Even though the Philharmonic was more prestigious, I adored our condutor,

Brother Dayley. He was kind, humble, and deeply artistic; he brought out the best in us.

I was glad to be a part of this exciting trip. The peak of our tour was to be a concert for the College Band Directors' National Association at the University of California, Berkeley. We all boarded one bus; the tympani, tubas, and other large instruments were loaded on a separate truck driven by two of the percussion players, one of whom was Mark Davenport, Sheryl's likable new boyfriend. Our first stop was Reno, Nevada, for a concert at the local LDS stake center that night.

When we arrived at the stake center that afternoon, a somber group of men came out to meet us. Brother Dayley stepped off to talk with them. When he got back on the bus, ashen-faced, he picked up the intercom speaker.

"I have bad news. The instrument truck overturned and burned on the way here. We don't know how Mark and Don are."

We all gasped; some cried. Poor Mark and Don! What about the tubas and percussion instruments and the sheet music? Brother Dayley led the band in prayer. Then we sat and waited while he went back into the stake center to make some calls.

Finally Brother Dayley returned. "I talked with Mark and Don at the stake center in Battle Mountain. They aren't hurt. Many of the instruments are burned, but miraculously, all our sheet music is okay. The guys had moved it to the back of the truck, and the fire was in the front.

"It happened a few miles outside of Battle Mountain. The fire department put it out, and the truck was towed back to town. As the guys were looking for a phone, they spotted some missionaries who helped them find some local members, and they called the music department.

"We've decided that they'll rent another truck and drive here tonight with what's left of the instruments. We won't play a concert tonight, but if we can borrow some replacement instruments, we'll go ahead with the tour starting tomorrow. Now let's go home with our host families."

Steve Rolandelli, a third percussion player, was from the San Francisco Bay area. He called home, and his father helped arrange to borrow instruments from the Air National Guard. Meanwhile, Mark and Don arrived during the night. They stayed with the bus while Steve and a band staff member drove off in the morning for San Francisco to round up instruments in time for the concert.

As the bus drove on to California, the musicians sang, shared testimonies, and prayed together. Even though I was the only Gentile in the band I felt welcome, not as an insider, but as an accepted outsider. My respect and affection grew for these devout, honorable Latter-day Saints.

When we arrived in Oakland, California, I was assigned with another band member to the home of Mr. and

Mrs. Carlson. During dinner, Mr. Carlson announced, "Eat heartily. Our Fast and Testimony meeting lasts until 6:30 tomorrow night."

The first Sunday of each month is Fast Sunday. To observe this day, Church members don't eat or drink for at least two consecutive meals, usually for about twenty-four hours. The purpose of this fast is to draw nearer to God, to strengthen the body against temptations, and to donate special fast offerings to the poor. Members attend a special Sunday Fast and Testimony Meeting instead of Sacrament Meeting.

Mrs. Carlson asked me about my own customs for Fast Sunday; was I accustomed to a light snack or drink of juice in the morning? I said, "I'm not a Latter-day Saint, but I will join you in fasting tomorrow."

"Oh!" A look of dismay flashed across Mrs. Carlson's face. "I'm so sorry. I'll fix you a meal tomorrow." She never expected BYU to send her a Gentile guest.

"Thank you anyway," I insisted, "but I prefer to fast with you tomorrow."

Mrs. Carlson never got over the shock of having me there, but her husband seized the opportunity. I didn't want to seem ungrateful for their hospitality, so I listened politely to his efforts to convert me.

After Sunday school in the morning, Mr. Carlson suggested that we forget our hunger by going to visit the

Oakland Temple. The Temple was mammoth, white, and surrounded by acres of gardens. The Temple itself was closed on Sunday, which didn't matter because non-members couldn't go inside anyway, and I was the whole point of the visit. What mattered was that the visitor's center was open.

In the visitor's center I saw photographs of the ornate rooms inside, in which were performed endowments, marriages for all eternity, sealings of family members for eternity, and baptisms for the dead. We also took the guided tour during which local missionaries presented the now-familiar story of Joseph Smith and the True Church.

After that we went to Fast and Testimony Meeting: more singing, the sacrament, and testimonies. I heard stomachs rumbling. The Carlsons hurried us home for dinner when it was over, and then we were whisked off to a fireside given in honor of the Wind Ensemble.

It was a day of Mormon overload—three LDS meetings with a temple visit in between. The next morning I withdrew to a back seat beside some instruments and read my Bible on the bus.

Sitting in the bus as we arrived at Berkeley for our big concert, we stared out the windows at the local students. With our dress and grooming code, did we ever look out of place!

The flute player in front of me said, "I kind of like

being a clean-cut weirdo."

"So do I," I answered.

Our beloved Brother Dayley often shared a devotional and led the band in prayer before a performance, but tonight, the night we'd been working toward for months, he spoke with deep conviction. "I would like to share my testimony with you. I know that God lives and has a body of flesh and bone, and I know that Jesus is the Christ. I know that Jesus Christ and our Heavenly Father appeared to Joseph Smith and that this is the restored Church on the earth today. I testify and believe with every bone and fiber of my body and soul that this is the True Church. I say these things in the name of Jesus Christ. Amen."

"Amen," echoed everyone solemnly.

Inspired by Brother Dayley's heartfelt testimony, the Wind Ensemble members played their hearts out. Even I felt inspired by the love and devotion of my fellow musicians. I loved them in return but wondered, would I be loved into their Church? I also wondered, could these millions of dear people be wrong?

Ever since I'd come to BYU, I had been too busy worrying about Mormonism to love Mormons. But spending a week in a bus with Saints who cared for me had softened my heart. I let down my guard around my LDS friends.

A week after I got back to Provo Janet said to me,

"Why don't you come watch us dance this afternoon? We're performing at the Language Training Mission.[8]" Janet was a member of a BYU traveling dance troupe, the "Latin American Folk Dancers," and they were dancing for the missionaries training to go to Spanish-speaking countries.

"Janet, I'm not allowed to go in there!" That old building on the edge of our campus was mysteriously off-limits to the students.

"I'm sure you can attend a performance there. Come on, I'll dress you up like a missionary so you won't look out of place."

We looked in my closet. Even though all my clothes conformed to BYU's dress code, none had that "sister missionary" look. "Let's see what I have," said Janet. She brought out a long skirt and jacket. "Try this on."

It fit. Janet tugged on the skirt and smoothed my collar. I tried to look serious and asked, "How do I look?"

"You look marvelous, Sister Avery!" She hugged me. "The program starts at four o'clock, but I have to go early. I'll see you there."

I approached the clandestine Language Training Mission just before four. Ignoring a sign that prohibited visitors from entering, I tried a door and found it unlocked. The hallways echoed in spite of my efforts to step lightly; I discreetly followed a pair of elders-in-training and wound up in a big room filled with chairs. I sat inconspicuously in the back, near the exit, and watched as pairs of elders and sister missionaries came in and sat down. Most were working hard to communicate in Spanish.

When the dancers came on stage in bright Latin costumes, I was relieved to see Janet. She winked at me, and I smiled back. The performance was festive, but I kept glancing at the missionaries around me. The audience was subdued—I sensed an air of disciplined excitement about the missionaries. When the program finished, everyone rose and walked quietly out. I tried to look solemn too as I slipped out the door. I breathed easier once I was outside and had checked my shoulder to make sure I wasn't being followed.

At dinner, Janet was eager to hear how I liked the program. "I loved it!" I said. "And thanks for inviting me."

"Oh, Carol, it was such a privilege for me to serve the Church by performing at the LTM. And to see all those handsome young men! They will make excellent husbands after their missions." Janet was still writing to her boyfriend on his mission in Germany.

"Returned missionaries are in demand here, aren't they?"

"Oh yes. I want to marry one. I mean, if an LDS guy hasn't gone on a mission, he really hasn't obeyed the Lord. Unless he's blind, or crippled, or something. But even members with special needs sometimes serve missions. And women too, but for us, it's a higher calling to get married. Then if we're still single by age twenty-one, we can go on a mission."

"You're supposed to get married by age twenty-one?"

"Well, not necessarily by age twenty-one, but marriage is a sacred duty in the Church. You see, having children provides mortal bodies for the spirits now waiting in the premortal existence. They have to be born into the world in order to progress toward godhood.

"Marriage is also part of our salvation. The Church leaders have told us that we cannot enter the Celestial Kingdom unless we have been married in the temple. In fact, we receive our spiritual fulfillment and rewards in the resurrection through our husband's priesthood."

"What happens to single women?"

"I don't know, but I wouldn't want to take any chances."

On our way out of the dining room we stopped to check our mailbox. Janet saw it first. "Hey, there's a package slip!"

We waited expectantly while the clerk retrieved it. "Oh, Carol, it's for you!" Janet said.

I opened the small package to find that my brother had sent me a New American Standard New Testament. Just then Joseph, an overbearing acquaintance of Janet's, came up. "Hi, Janet. Hi, Carol. Hey, you got a package! What is it?"

"It's a book from my brother." I smiled hesitantly.

"Let's see it." He looked inside. "I thought it looked like a Bible. Carol, this isn't the King James Version. I know you aren't LDS, but don't you know that the King James is the most accurate version?"

"I *do* know King James is all you use." I was annoyed.

Janet and I walked quietly back to our dorm room. I didn't really expect any sympathy from her. She cleared her throat and said, "Sorry, Carol. But he was right."

"I knew you would agree with him."

I kept my new Bible to myself and in public used only the King James Version. I decided that the battle over translations wasn't so important. It was true; the King James Version was accurate, but so was the New American Standard, and I liked reading a translation I could understand.

I was fortunate to be in Brother Turner's second semester music theory class. Sheryl and I were in there together, and we did interesting class projects like composing an operetta based on the James Thurber story, "The Unicorn in the Garden."

One day, to develop our musical ears, Brother Turner named a hymn and asked us to write down the melody and chord changes from memory. The first was a common Mormon hymn that was set to the tune of the familiar "What a Friend We Have in Jesus." I got that one, but I'd never heard of the second hymn he named. I wrote on my paper, "I don't know this one; I'm not LDS," handed it in, and sat back down in my seat.

Brother Turner looked at my paper and then looked at me with such great tenderness in his eyes that I had to look away. The next time we did that exercise, he chose "Jingle Bells" and "Silent Night."

As for religion class, I hadn't signed up for it this semester. Nobody came along and made me, so avoidance worked, at least in the short run.

I was also taking modern dance. There had been dozens of dance classes among the hundreds of P.E. classes to choose from in the class schedule; I chose modern dance. I thought I looked awful in a leotard, and I wasn't very graceful, but in the locker room I did get to sneak some peeks at the married women's temple garments. It was rather anticlimactic, and I didn't talk about it.

In preparing to host that convention for Baptist students from Utah and Idaho, Diane had arranged the program and speakers with the regional BSU director. I arranged for BYU Food Services to cater a banquet on Friday evening. We scheduled time for a campus tour. Members of our church had volunteered to host the visiting students in their homes.

The morning of our convention, BYU's newspaper, *The Daily Universe*, ran a story about us. According to the article, ours was the first-ever non-LDS religious convention held at BYU. Reporters interviewed Pastor Don Plott, who reassured them that the Baptists were not coming to proselytize, only to meet together. We also noticed another front-page story, a notice about a lecture concerning the Pearl of Great Price to be given that evening in the room next to ours by Hugh Nibley, one of the foremost LDS scholars.

Before dinner, carloads of students arrived at the BYU student center. We welcomed them heartily and recognized many from the fall meeting. The students were awed by our tour of campus, which we embellished with anecdotes about life at BYU. One commented, "You're surrounded by Mormonism—from the statue of Brigham Young to the quotations etched on the walls of buildings! It's everywhere! Don't you wonder sometimes whether there might be something to it all?"

Frankly, I did wonder sometimes. The Church looked so good and it was so powerful that it was hard not to join the crowd.

Soon after the convention, it was time to get ready for finals. And then, my first full year at Brigham Young University was over! I went back to Phoenix to get a summer job and gather strength to tackle another year at BYU.

chapter seven

*D*uring the summer Diane, upbeat as always, called me at home. "Carol, you'll never believe this. Someone from the BYU Centennial Committee called. They're putting on a big homecoming show this year, and they invited the BSU to enter a float in the Homecoming Parade! As soon as we come up with a theme that relates to BYU history or United States history, the men at church will help us build it."

"Okay, I'll think about it. Say, Diane, I'm coming back by bus in a couple of weeks. Can you pick me up at the bus station?"

I told my pastor in Phoenix about the float and he said, "You ought to do it on religious freedom in America. You know, Roger Williams, one of the original settlers, was a Baptist." By the time I got on the bus for Provo, I was sure that religious freedom was the right theme for our float.

During the past year, Sheryl, my horn-playing friend from Phoenix, and I had continued promising each other that we'd be roommates, but by the end of the spring we wanted Janet to room with us too. The solution was easy: we decided to move into Heritage Halls, a set of apartment buildings on campus. Each apartment had three bedrooms, a kitchen, and a bathroom to be shared by six girls, so Janet had recruited three other girls (all LDS, of course) to fill up our apartment. BYU provided this housing as an opportunity for students to develop skills in cooking and homemaking, and we were expected to eat meals together and share domestic chores. Before the summer break, we'd met to decide who would bring which household items, so I had packed my grandmother's old pots and pans.

I was the BSU president again, and Dawnena had agreed to be the vice-president. I remembered how I felt one year before—scared and lonely. Now I felt optimistic. Maybe I could make a difference this year for some other new students.

When my bus rolled into Provo, I called Diane. "Dawnena's over here and we're fixing lunch," she said. "I'll be right there."

"Whoa, Carol! What a suntan!" Dawn said when she saw me.

"Yeah, that's Phoenix all right. But look at you. You always have a tan. It's not fair."

After lunch, Diane said, "Either of you have any ideas for the float?"

"I think we should do it on religious freedom," I said.

"No kidding! I've been thinking the same thing," Diane exclaimed. "That must be the one!" But Diane had plans for more than a float in the parade. "As for our regular meetings, I think more people would come if we met during the day. All we need is a room in the Wilkinson Center, and we can have brown bag lunches and Bible study every week."

"We need publicity right away, so other Gentiles can find us before they become LDS."

"Not posters, though. Remember?" Dawnena had helped make those posters that vanished.

Diane said, "We have some money to put an ad in the *Daily Universe*. Dawn, you're a communications major. Will you take care of that?"

"Sure."

The next day I re-registered our club at the Organizations Office and scheduled a room. Dawn had an ad in the paper by Friday, and she, Diane, Liz and I held our first meeting the next Tuesday at noon. Three new people showed up. Jackie, a freshman, was LDS but her boyfriend back home was Baptist. They had made a deal to learn about each other's churches. Joel Miller, with sandy blond hair and a great suntan, was at the Y on a tennis scholarship. He hadn't been a Christian for long, he said, and that morning on the tennis court saw a copy of the paper with our ad. He was relieved to meet some "ordinary Christians."

The third visitor looked more mature and serious than the rest of us. He had a receding hairline and wore a tie, which to me was taking the dress code a bit far. "I'm Bob Clark," he said. "I'm a Methodist, but I haven't found any Methodists here yet. I visited your church on Sunday. I came from Indiana to get my master's in business."

I was so excited to meet these new Gentiles that I became determined to "search and rescue" even more. At Deseret Towers, I explained who I was and asked about a list of Baptist students.

The clerk laughed and said, "No, but would you like to look through the resident cards?" She motioned toward two drawers full of three-by-five cards. I was surprised to have access to them, and browsed for an hour, looking at the "religious preference" line. I copied down the names and room numbers of the few not listed "LDS."

As much as I loathed knocking on strangers' doors, I was a girl on a mission. When the first door opened, I asked for Susan, who had identified herself as "Christian."

"I'm Susan."

I explained who I was, and she said to her roommate, "Hey, guess what. Someone's here from the Baptist Student Union."

They looked at me the way some people must look

at Mormon missionaries at their door. I left my name and number and went on to Helaman Halls.

Jane, a freckled redhead, answered the door there. When I introduced myself, she said in a drawl, "Y'all are from the Baptist Student Union? Really? I'm from Waco, Texas! We have a big BSU down there. I'm so glad you came! I was fixin' to go look for another Baptist that I heard lives downstairs, but I keep puttin' it off."

"Let's go together," I said. We stopped at the front desk, and I asked the clerk if she knew a Baptist girl on the first floor.

"Are you *Baptists?* Hey, I heard there's a Baptist club here," she said. "Let me see if I can find a Baptist on the first floor." I looked at Jane and smiled. "Yes, here it is. Nancy Barnes, Room 1107."

"Thanks for your help!" I said. Jane and I walked down to Room 1107 and found the door ajar.

"Hello, Nancy?" I looked in.

"Nancy's down the hall washing her hair. She'll be right back," her roommate said.

Soon Nancy came along with a towel wrapped around her head. She looked at her roommate and then said to us, "Are you here to see me?"

When I told her who we were, she said, "Praise the Lord! I wanted to find some Christians!"

We talked happily, and then Jane and Nancy went

off to the dining hall together. As I left, I offered to find both girls a ride to church on Sunday and a picnic afterwards.

Along with Jane and Nancy, Bob and Joel showed up again, and one other girl came in a taxi. After church we carpooled up to Sundance, a nearby ski resort, which in early September made the perfect picnic area. We cooked out, threw Frisbees, and I watched the newcomers talk eagerly with each other as I had done the year before. We came down the mountain in time to attend a gathering for non-Mormons sponsored by the Catholic Church. About fifty students came, and I was surprised to see the graduate assistant from one of my music classes. Larry looked like a graduate student—bookish, and definitely not athletic.

"Hi Larry!" I said. "You're not LDS?"

"Your name's Carol, right? You aren't either?"

"No, in fact I'm the president of the Baptist Student Union." I invited Larry to our Tuesday meeting.

Larry liked it and kept coming back and one night he took me to dinner. He said, "I've been spending time with all of you, and there's something special about you—some kind of sparkle. What can you tell me about your faith?"

I told him about my relationship with God and handed him a gospel tract. Larry ate in silence, completely absorbed in the reading. Finally he said, "Yes. This is exactly what I need. I don't know how I never figured it out before. Can I take this booklet home?"

The next morning in class, Larry was radiant. He said, "I feel like a new man."

"You are!"

"Carol," Sheryl reminded me from her bed early one morning, "we have to cook dinner tonight."

Our new roommates Becky, Barbara, and Julie, all from the Salt Lake City area, turned out to be fine friends for Sheryl, Janet, and me. According to our new cooking schedule, tonight was Sheryl's and my first night to cook dinner for the "family." That afternoon we walked to the nearest grocery store.

"What should we cook?" she wondered on the way.

"I don't know. Let's see what's on sale when we get to the store."

In the meat section I exclaimed, "Look how cheap this chicken is!"

"Wow. But do you know how to cook it? It says 'stewing chicken' on the label."

"Well, it's a whole chicken. My mom used to just bake these in the oven and carve them at the table."

"Okay." Little Bo Peep was not one to argue.

We bought the chicken, some potatoes, two cans of corn, and a cake mix. By the time we carried it all home, our arms were killing us, so we sat down to rest before cooking. I sprinkled salt and pepper on the chicken and put it in the oven, and we worked together on the rest of the meal.

At six o'clock, the roommates gathered in the kitchen. "Umm! Smells great in here! What's for dinner?" asked Barbara.

"Chicken and potatoes," we answered proudly. I set the chicken on the table, and we thanked God for the food. It didn't cut very easily, but I managed to chop off a chunk for each roommate. I took my first bite. I had never tried to eat anything as tough and gristly as that chicken.

I glanced around the table. Everyone was smiling. "Umm, tastes good," said Becky.

"My piece is hard to chew," I ventured. "Is anyone else's?"

Everyone agreed that it was hard to chew, but it smelled really great and looked good too. "It's okay," said Becky. "My jaw needed the exercise."

We six roommates grew so close, eating each other's cooking every night, that one day Julie said, "I have an idea. Since we're like a family, why don't we meet for family prayer every day, like we do at home?"

"Good thinking!" Janet exclaimed.

I was quiet. I was managing well enough with five LDS roommates, but I still didn't feel like praying aloud with them. My roommates were as sincere as I was, but I wasn't comfortable praying aloud, given the wide divide in our theology.

Janet said, "Carol, with all your Baptist activities, you are probably the busiest of all of us. When would be the best time for you?" Everyone looked at me.

"Oh, don't arrange around me. Just go ahead even if I can't make it."

I had been through this last year with Janet over Family Home Evening, but she still hadn't given up, and now she got support from the new roommates. Avoidance wasn't working.

"No, Carol, we can't have it without you! It's not the same unless everyone is there," Julie insisted.

"Okay." I was cornered. "How about right before dinner? That's when we're all together anyway," I said, hoping to keep family prayer confined to the dinner blessing.

"I think that first thing in the morning would be a great way to start our day," said Barbara."

I believe Sheryl was on my side when she quietly said, "I leave early every morning to practice horn before class. I try to get there by 6:00."

Janet solved that one quickly. "Oh, so we'll have to meet about 5:45, won't we?"

I was sure someone would protest, but Becky, the last one to speak, said, "I guess some of us could go back to bed afterward."

"Okay, then it's settled. Let's start tomorrow morning. We can take turns leading it; I'll start." Janet was serious about her quest for the Celestial Kingdom. She wanted to do everything *right.*

The next morning, Sheryl gently touched my shoulder. "Carol," she whispered, "it's a quarter till six. Sorry to wake you, but it's time for prayer."

I stumbled into the kitchen to see my other roommates looking sleepy, kneeling on the floor. I sat on a chair, bowed my head, and my eyes fell shut.

"Let's all kneel as we pray," Janet said. She meant me, since everyone else was already kneeling. I got down on my knees too.

"Our dear Heavenly Father," she began, "we thy daughters come before Thee humbly this morning to ask Thy blessing on us this day. We ask Thee to bless our daily lives and our schoolwork so that we may do well and be pleasing unto Thee.

"Heavenly Father, we also beseech Thee on behalf of the leadership of this Thy Church. We know the great responsibility Thou hast placed upon them, and we ask Thee to strengthen our Prophet and give him physical health and wisdom to speak Thy word."

Janet prayed on for the apostles and missionaries, and then prayed, "Father, we would ask Thee to open the eyes and hearts of those who have not seen the light of the everlasting gospel. We pray that Thou wouldst remove the veil from their minds so they would realize and accept the truth of Thy Church. We know this is Thy plan for our exaltation and our return to Thy presence. We say these things in the name of Thy Son, Jesus Christ. Amen."

"Amen," echoed everyone.

I crawled back into bed and couldn't sleep. Here I was again, caught in a miserable situation because I didn't have the resolve to say no. It felt like five against one, or at least four and a half; Sheryl was partly on my side.

That afternoon Becky stuck her head into my room and said, "Carol, I hope we don't impose on you too much, since you aren't LDS. If I were you, I'd feel intimidated. We want you to find the truth of the gospel because we care so much about you."

"I know. Thanks, Becky."

"I'd feel pretty alone if I were in your shoes."

Maybe Becky was an ally too. Her empathy did my heart good.

Larry, the graduate assistant, stopped showing up at our weekly Bible study, and after class one day I asked him about it.

"It's my roommates. They're returned missionaries, and they pester me constantly about their church."

"I know what you mean. Mine do too, but Larry, we don't have to listen to them." I tried to ignore the obvious hypocrisy of me telling Larry how to handle his roommates.

He called me a week later. Sounding thoroughly discouraged, he said, "Carol, I hope you wouldn't mind if I joined the Mormon Church."

"Mind? If you joined the Church?"

"I think my life would be easier. And cheaper, of course. The Church is everything here. I'm tired of fighting it."

"Larry, wait a while. Don't jump into it yet, okay?"

"Okay."

It was easy for me to say, but I was still stuck on my own problem. I didn't want to alienate my kind and well-intentioned roommates, but praying aloud with them made me really unhappy. I couldn't live with the compromise forever; I needed to go one way or the other.

One day, Bob Clark took me aside. "Carol, I have a bone to pick with you."

"With me? You do?" I liked Bob a lot; he was good-natured and sensible.

"Yes. You're the BSU president. And I'm tired of listening to all the criticism of Mormons. You criticize what they believe, what they do and say, and even what they wear. What if an LDS friend walked in here and heard it? It's not polite. It's not very Christian, either."

Yikes. It was that old bad habit, but I hardly noticed it anymore. I didn't connect cynicism about the religion with the friends whom I (most of the time anyway) loved. But I listened carefully the next time we were together. It was true. There was a wisecrack about Heavenly Mother, and one about sainthood. There were war stories from religion classes.

When I talked with Diane about it, she said, "People mock what they fear. I think we ridicule the Church because we're so overwhelmed by it."

"But Bob's right. It's not very Christian. What can we do?"

"First, thank God that Bob brought it up. Awareness is a big step toward overcoming the problem. And if fear is at the root of it, we can pray for courage. And for kind hearts."

Diane and I prayed, and I spoke up at the next meeting. The group listened silently, then became prayerful and repentant. We knew we needed a safe place to talk about the stress of life here, but everyone agreed that cynicism was not appropriate. We pledged to hold each other accountable for our speech. After that, when a person accidentally made a smart remark, someone else gave that person a Knowing Look.

Then Janet left a five-page letter, handwritten in her curly script, on my desk. She wrote that she knew the Church was true, and she challenged me to pray with an open mind and ask the Holy Ghost to reveal the truth to me. She was concerned for me and said that she was accountable before God if she didn't tell me these things. She urged me not to rush to my Baptist friends with this challenge, but to accept it from her and from God with an open mind. She pledged that if I found it to be untrue, she and millions of Saints would leave the Church.

She closed with this: "I promise you, dear sister, that if you pray to God with an open mind and ask Him if what I have said is true, you will have a good feeling come over you and the Holy Ghost will bear witness to its truthfulness....I also guarantee that you will never rest the same if you deny the feelings you receive....Now the weight is on you to test it and prove it to yourself."

The next day Janet was alone in her room. I knocked and said, "Thank you for your letter. I know it comes from a sincere heart."

With relief in her eyes, she said, "Oh Carol, I hope I didn't make you angry. You know, I *had* to write that letter. I am responsible before God and had to put that responsibility on you. I don't want to be blamed if you miss eternal salvation. Please consider what I wrote."

"I will, Janet."

The next day I was ironing in the laundry room when Brother Calkins came in. Brother Calkins and his wife were the resident assistants of our building. He said casually, "I noticed that you are not a member of the Church. That's interesting."

"Yes, it is. There aren't many non-members around here."

He said, "I wasn't raised in the Church. I used to be a Nazarene and didn't find any meaning there, so later I became a Catholic. That wasn't right either, and then through a series of miraculous events, I found the Church. It has changed my life."

"I became a Christian about two years ago. It has changed my life, too."

Brother Calkins said, "Carol, you will join the Church. All good people do."

All good people join the Church?

I had decided against Mormonism before I ever came to the Y. But now Janet's letter got me thinking. I had never honestly accepted that challenge. Was I afraid to ask God to show me which church to choose, as Joseph Smith had asked long ago?

It was so confusing here that sometimes I wondered whether God was real at all. How could I be right and all these people wrong? But I knew I couldn't have it both ways—it was either the Mormon God or the God of the Bible, not both. The Gods were too different.

Come on, I thought, these doubts were ridiculous. I was a devoted Christian, the president of the Baptist Student Union. God was at work in my life all the time, providing encouragement from the Bible and from Christian friends, wasn't he? I had seen God work a miracle in our hearts just recently, setting us free from a bad habit. But was I being honest with myself? Did I really want to know the truth? As usual, I went outside to walk and pray. "Okay, Lord, I feel a little silly having waited so long, but I am asking you if the Mormon Church is true. I know that if you show me it is true, I'll have to obey and join the Church. I don't know how I'd explain that to Diane and Dawn, though. You'd have to help me. Thank you that I can trust you. Amen."

I walked for a long time. I listened, and waited, and listened. I walked and walked. I didn't feel any burning in my bosom. But the more I listened, the more I was convinced that truth was not about feeling a burning in the bosom anyway. Truth had to conform to actual facts and reality, and the Bible was a trustworthy, historically verifiable book. Archeology and external sources supported the Bible, and not the Book of Mormon.[9] And the Bible said that Jesus was the way, the truth, and the life, and that we didn't need another gospel.

I walked some more. I wanted to be sure. The more

I kept listening and praying, the more I knew that I could trust what the Bible says about spiritual matters. It was getting dark when I finally went home and knocked on Janet's bedroom door. "Janet," I said, "I did it. I accepted your challenge."

"And?" She was bursting with anticipation.

"I still don't think the Church is true; I still accept the Bible as my only authority. I'm sorry to disappoint you, my friend. And also, I'm not going to get up for family prayer anymore. It's just not right for me."

It was October, time to press on with the homecoming float. To illustrate our theme of "religious freedom," we decided to build an old-time country church structure and attend "Sunday meeting" on the float. Liz would dress in her Chinese outfit, Victor in African dress, Dawn in Native American clothes, and the rest of us would wear pioneer outfits. We rented a float bed, and some skilled carpenters in the church built an altar and small pews. Sheryl, Becky, and Julie even helped me build a stained glass window out of colored plastic for the front of the church. Although I didn't own a pioneer outfit myself, Janet agreed to loan me hers. Most Latter-day Saints have pioneer outfits; Pioneer Day is a big holiday in Utah every July, and everybody dresses up in calico and sunbonnets.

We assembled the float in a warehouse. The result

was a handsome little church with a stained glass window, three pairs of small pews, and a pulpit boasting a large white cross. The manager of the local Lincoln Mercury dealership loaned us a courtesy Continental to tow the float, and the director of Utah and Idaho BSU ministries, Guy Ward, came down from Salt Lake City to drive it.

At seven in the morning, I arrived at the starting site as Diane and Guy drove up towing our float. As we climbed on, Diane's face was flushed. She said, "Carol, we are so lucky. The church frame was almost too tall for the door of the warehouse. I thought for sure that the top would get smashed off. Oh Carol, you should have seen it! I prayed and prayed; I think God helped it clear the doorway."

As the parade marched down University Avenue, we waved and sang bravely along with a tape of old-time gospel hymns. The streets were packed with spectators, many of whom applauded as we rode by. When we were in front of the dignitaries' grandstand, the parade paused to take up slack. I heard applause and turned to see Dallin Oaks, the president of BYU, and Spencer W. Kimball, the president of the LDS Church, smiling and waving. We waved back and kept singing our hymns.

Afterwards, Diane returned to the warehouse where the float would be disassembled. She called me that afternoon. "Carol, guess what! As we towed the float back in through that very same doorway, the top of the church was smashed off!"

Someone later theorized that the tires of the trailer had warmed up and inflated while driving. Whatever the scientific explanation was, I knew that God had looked after our little float.

chapter eight

I was sitting in orchestra rehearsal, counting measures of rest and looking at the back of the clarinet players' heads. I already knew most of the woodwind players, but there were a few new backs of heads to look at this year. Now I was playing horn along with Sheryl in the Philharmonic Orchestra. It was a busy fall; the orchestra recorded the soundtrack for a centennial musical and performed live at gala events.

During the break I met the front of one of those heads. David, a clarinet player, was just back from his mission to Uruguay. He had gone there after his freshman year, and was now picking up school where he'd left off two years earlier. David was tall and slim, and his glasses gave him an intellectual look. Not surprisingly, he seemed very mature.

We chatted again during the next rehearsal, and the next. David was fun to talk with. Having spoken Spanish constantly for two years, he loved to spice up his speech with Spanish expressions. Because of my classes in Spanish, I usually understood him and answered back in Spanish. David took to calling me *Señorita Cornista* (Miss Horn Player).

One afternoon, as we packed up after rehearsal, David said, "I have to teach Family Home Evening tonight, but I haven't prepared the lesson yet. Do you teach sometimes too?"

"I used to, but I don't go to Family Home Evening anymore."

"You don't? Shame on you. Why not?"

"I'm not LDS."

David stopped with a piece of his clarinet in each hand. "I didn't know that." He turned and searched me with his eyes. "May I ask what you are?"

"I'm a Christian. I go to the Baptist church."

David closed his instrument case and said, "I would like to come visit your church. Mine ends at five on Sundays. Do you have an evening meeting?"

"We have evening church at six o'clock."

I was sure he wouldn't come. Latter-day Saints came to our church only if they had an assignment from a religion class. But just before six on Sunday afternoon, I saw David bicycle into the church parking lot. I walked outside to meet him.

"*Hola, Señor,*" I said.

"*Hola, Señorita.*"

"*Bienvenidos a mi iglesia.* (Welcome to my church.)"

"*Gracias.*"

David sat beside me during the service. He tried to sing along with the hymns and didn't attempt to correct any of our doctrines. He was good company.

I walked with David out to his bicycle after the service. "Thanks for coming, David," I said. "Why did you, anyway?"

He shrugged. "I just wanted to see what it was like. Hope that's okay. You're kind of rare here, you know."

David was in my music theory class too. Before the midterm exam he caught up with me after class and said, "Would you like to study together for the test?"

"Just us?"

"What do you think?"

"Sure."

We met in a practice room that evening. David played chord progressions on the piano, and I had to write down what he played. I kept up with him even on the secondary dominant chords, but he tricked me a couple of times with augmented and diminished chords.

Then it was my turn. I wasn't as good on the piano as David was, but I played two separate notes on the piano and had him guess the melodic interval between them. I got the giggles playing intervals that were several octaves apart, but he guessed most of them right.

When we were finished, David played and sang some of his favorite songs from Uruguay. He didn't talk to me at all about the Church.

I lay awake that night thinking about the fun time with him, and the next morning, I spent a long time deciding what to wear. On my way to orchestra I stopped in the restroom to make sure I looked okay.

The long rehearsal passed quickly as I listened to David lead the clarinet section. Whenever he glanced back, our eyes locked before we turned back to our music. I'm sure Sheryl noticed. She looked at me askance but never one to interfere, said nothing.

I didn't talk to any of my BSU friends about David. I didn't want to make something out of what was probably nothing, but it felt like a big secret was growing in my heart.

Another Sunday evening, one of the senior adults in the church hurried up to me and said, "Carol, a new college student just walked in. Come and meet him."

As I approached, he said, "Hi. I'm Tom Murphy. I was passing by and saw some lights on, so I decided to check it out. I'm a student at the Y."

"So am I. Are you a Christian?"

"Well, I'm LDS right now. I hope I'm still welcome."

"Of course."

Tom sat with Dawnena and me in the service. I wanted to find out what he meant by being a Mormon "right now," so afterwards we invited him out for a bite to eat. Over French fries and Dr Pepper, Tom told his story.

"I was raised in a Christian family, but in high school I met this girl who was a zealous Mormon. She loved her church and wanted me to visit with her. Finally last year I took those missionary lessons. The elders had a logical answer for every question I asked. They proved their case, and I was baptized.

"When I joined the LDS Church my mom cried a lot. I felt bad. In order to get away from home, I decided to come to Provo for school. I like BYU a lot, but the more I study religion here, the more questions I have."

"I like it here too, except for religion class," I said.

Tom continued, "Then I heard about this big book written by Jerald and Sandra Tanner, and I got a copy. Have you heard of them?"

"Oh, yes! The famous former Mormons, with a bookstore down the street from the Salt Lake Temple."

"I read about all the changes in the Book of Mormon. I read about Joseph Smith's background with Masonry and magic. And about the Egyptian papyri that Joseph supposedly translated into the Book of Abraham, but they were really just Egyptian funeral texts. And about the secrecy in the Church, and things like that.

"The more I read, the more foolish I felt for joining the Church, but it's hard to leave when you live in Provo and attend BYU. I have five housemates, and they're all returned missionaries. They harass me because I don't attend the branch anymore. By the way, if you ever call my house, don't tell them you're Baptists."

"We won't," said Dawnena.

"Whatever happened to your girlfriend?" I asked.

"She's dating someone else."

"How's your Christian faith?"

"It's all coming back to me. I'm sure my mom has never stopped praying."

Dawnena said, "Why don't you transfer to another university?"

"I'm going to. I've already applied to a Christian university in Oklahoma."

On the way home, Dawnena said, "Poor Tom, living with five returned missionaries."

"Hey Dawn, speaking of returned missionaries, I want to talk with you about something."

"Okay."

"Someone, actually."

She was quiet.

"Remember that friend of mine who visited our church? I've been studying with him."

"That clarinet player? He seemed really nice."

"He *is* really nice."

"Is it romantic?"

"No. Well, I don't know. How could it be romantic? He's a *returned missionary*. But I can't stop thinking about him."

"Do you think he thinks about you?"

"Probably."

"He'll never ask you out. You know what the Church says: 'every date is a potential mate,' and they're not supposed to date Gentiles."

"Does studying together count as going out?"

"Apparently he doesn't think so."

"Dawn, this guy is just so easy to be with. We have so much in common. He doesn't try to pressure me at all."

"You and I know lots of girls who joined the Church for a boyfriend."

"I'm not going to join the Church. But I see David every day in class, and sometimes twice a day. And I really like him. Dawn, what am I going to do?"

"Well, it's almost Christmas vacation. Just get through the semester without doing anything dumb."

It was a relief to go home for Christmas, but I still couldn't stop thinking about David. I replayed the jokes we had shared. His handsome face and figure were imprinted in my mind, and I heard his music in my sleep. But

I didn't talk to anyone at home about him. I returned to BYU in January resolved to get this wonderful, handsome Mormon out of my heart, and get my life back to normal. I first saw David in the bookstore.

"Hi, Carol!" My resolve melted at the sound of his kind voice. We compared our class schedules. David was in two of my classes as well as orchestra, so we'd be together daily again.

I looked forward to music theory, acoustics, and orchestra practice. I started waking up earlier to have more time in the morning. I even wore some makeup—not like I did in junior high, but just enough to make me feel prettier.

Sheryl, while keeping up with all her homework and hours of music practice, was still dating Mark, the survivor of the truck fire. Once in a while Mark came over to eat our cooking. Mark and Sheryl were a perfect match, like Jack and Jill, like Raggedy Ann and Andy, like Donny and Marie. Their happiness was enviable.

One night after the light was off Sheryl asked me, "We have our first theory test next week. Are you going to study with anyone?"

I was afraid she would hear my heart pounding. "I don't know." After a moment I said, "Why do you ask?"

"I was just wondering."

Janet was still writing to her missionary diligently every Sunday, but she hadn't been receiving many letters from Germany. She didn't rush to check the mail anymore.

When I asked her about it, she said, "I know he's busy from morning till night with missionary work, but people do change while they're on missions, especially overseas. Maybe he has changed. It's okay. If it doesn't work out maybe I'll meet another RM [returned missionary]."

But for me, one RM was one too many. I was failing in my determined efforts to forget about David. I just couldn't think straight about him. I realized that the few quiet times I'd had with God lately had been spent praying that something would work out with David. I was so unrealistic I even prayed for him to leave the Church. My heart was in conflict with itself.

Then one Sunday morning in church, we sang the hymn, "I Surrender All." The words penetrated my soul: "All to Jesus I surrender, all to him I freely give....I will ever love and trust him, in his presence daily live. All to Jesus I surrender, humbly at his feet I bow, worldly pleasures all forsaken: take me, Jesus, take me now...." By the fourth verse, I was wiping tears from my eyes.

We sat down and I listened to a sermon about people who "tell God to leave them alone." The pastor said that even Christians who want to live lives of devotion might have hidden areas of resistance to God.

"Are you talking to me, God?" I wondered. "Does this mean me?"

I was sure that this meant me. That afternoon off by myself I prayed, "Lord, I have been hanging on to this relationship with David. I surrender it to you now; please have your way with me. Please help me to follow you."

I called Dawnena. "I'm giving it up," I said. "This thing with David. I've asked God to set me free from it."

"Good work, Carol."

"I need moral support."

"You got it."

Even though I had asked for God's help, I didn't expect it all to change overnight. I woke up the next morning braced for another day of fighting my feelings. But that heavy longing in my heart seemed to be gone; my thoughts about David were gentle, not obsessive.

The real test came when I walked into music theory class. I smiled at David and waved a little wave. He smiled back. I was glad to see him, but my heart didn't fall out of my chest like before.

I was thankful for this emotional freedom, but I still didn't think I was strong enough to spend time with David alone. I promised Dawn that I'd make some excuse if he invited me to study with him. I waited and waited, but David never asked me again all semester. We were still friendly, but the crush was gone. Later, I almost wondered whether I'd dreamed the whole thing up. But I knew God had worked a miracle in my heart, and apparently in David's heart, too.

I still saw Larry, the teaching assistant in my music class, and sometimes I'd whisper to him, "Still a Gentile?" So far he still nodded yes.

One day I decided to introduce Larry to Tom Murphy, that other friend with returned missionary problems. So I did, and they had a chat. The next time I saw Larry he said, "I'm going somewhere else for this master's degree. I don't know where yet, but this is my last semester at here. And I won't become a Mormon."

Our beloved pastor Don Plott, after several years of service in Provo, had "answered the call" to another church, and we began the search for a new pastor. Before long, a young Bible scholar from Texas, Phil McKown, took the position and moved to Provo with his wife and daughter.

Once he was settled, I offered to take him on a tour of campus. First we stopped in at the Wilkinson Center. Phil said, "Let's sit down so you can tell me all about the BSU. Where do we get a cup of coffee?"

I laughed and said, "Not here!"

"Oh, I keep forgetting. What do these people drink anyway?"

"Root beer, lemonade, orange soda, even hot chocolate. Anything the Church declares to be free of caffeine."

We found an empty table in the noisy dining area,

and I told Phil about the BSU, all the way up to what I'd just read in a letter from my sister Nancy. Now a high school senior herself, she heard a BYU recruiter say, "And for all you non-Mormons, we have an active Baptist student group on campus."

"How about that!" he said, "Free publicity!" Phil paused thoughtfully. "It seems to me that there must be a better way to reach these non-Mormon students. Maybe we can get that list of Baptist students earlier in the fall. October is way too late. There are several matters I'd like to talk with the university president about. What's his name again, Oaks?"

"Yeah, Dallin Oaks. I bet he'd love to hear from you!"

Phil changed the subject. "Carol, you're a sopho-more. Are you going to stay here till you graduate?"

"I have a four-year scholarship."

"Do you like it here?"

"It took some getting used to. But now I love my classes and my friends, and I have some awesome profes-sors. It feels like home. The one thing I can't figure out is how to get around those fourteen lousy credits of religion."

"You have to take fourteen credits of religion?"

"Yeah, to graduate you do. That's two credits times seven semesters. My first one drove me crazy, and I've avoided them ever since. So now I'd have to double up on religion classes to graduate on time."

"If you left here, where would you go?"

"I don't know. There's a famous music school in Texas. Living in the Bible belt sounds awfully good right now."

"Texas isn't heaven, you know."

But I couldn't shake the thought of changing schools. Just to check the school out, I wrote to request a catalog from North Texas State University. If I were to leave, I'd need a scholarship to replace the one I had, or at least to reduce the high out-of-state tuition rates.

I needed my Teacher again. I returned to that verse in Isaiah 30 from the pew Bible in Phoenix: "Your eyes will behold your Teacher, and your ears will hear a word behind you, 'This is the way, walk in it' whenever you turn to the right or to the left." I trusted the Lord to guide me by providing a scholarship, or by somehow solving that religion class problem.

The national Baptist student organization had arranged for a team of five students to come to BYU from Howard Payne University in Texas on their spring break "mission trip." Diane and I saw great potential in having five enthusiastic students spend a week with us. We decided that they could spend most of their time visiting international students and distributing Gideon New Testaments, courtesy of deacon Ben Rivera. Diane even asked permission for the team to distribute Bibles in the Wilkinson Center. We also wanted the students to experience Utah, so we scheduled a trip to Temple Square in Salt Lake City and planned for the team members to attend the BYU weekly devotional.

After their thousand-mile trip, the five students tumbled out of a large black car into our Sunday evening worship service. Tom, the team leader, was accompanied by John, a lanky African-American student, and three women. Our Jane, who was from Texas, could have kept them talking all night, but we sent them off to homes of First Baptist Church families.

We BYU students weren't on spring break that week, but in between classes we joined the Help Team members in visiting dozens of international students, delivering Bibles and inviting them to our weekly brown bag Bible study.

The team was scheduled to pass out New Testaments in the Wilkinson Center on Thursday morning. I sat through my class, wondering how the Bible distribution adventure was going. By eleven o'clock, the team was supposed to be at the KBYU studio in time for Tom's interview on Victor's program, *Religion Today*. I hurried over to the studio and found the team members talking excitedly.

Tom turned to me and said, "Oh Carol, are we glad

to see you! We're over there handing out New Testaments, and some man stomps up and says, 'Who are you, and why are you distributing literature on our campus?'

"I say, 'We're with the Baptist Student Union, and we have university approval to hand out these Bibles here today.'

"He says, 'Where is the faculty sponsor in charge of this group?

"I say, 'I'm sorry, but the sponsor is teaching and the club president is attending class.' I'm trying to be polite, you know, not make waves, but I'm starting to get nervous. Wishing you'd show up."

"He says, 'You stop handing out these materials and come with me right now!' But we're supposed to be over here at eleven.

"So John says to the guy, 'Sir, some of us have an important appointment at 11:00. May I go with you myself?' And the guy takes John with him!"

Ann, usually a quiet member of the team, clasped her hands to her heart and said, "John was the sacrifice for all of us!"

"So where's John now?" I asked.

"Here I am!" John sauntered up behind us with a gigantic grin on his face. "It's cool."

We crowded around him. "What happened?" Tom asked.

"That guy was so mad! He insisted over and over that this was a private institution and we had no right to be here. 'University policy prohibits distribution of tracts,' he kept saying. I kept telling him that we got permission."

I asked, "Did you ever figure out who he was?"

"No, I never did. He took me over to the administration building, but we never actually went in to see anyone. Finally he cooled off, and I promised we wouldn't give out any more Bibles. Of course, we were almost out of them anyway. That was all. He let me go, and here I am." John was still a little out of breath as he talked.

Victor appeared. "Tom, you're on camera in seven minutes."

"Okay," Tom said. "Whew, I'm a little nervous."

"I know," I sympathized. "I did this last year. But it's really easy once you get started." I was a big sophomore now.

Tom was escorted to a seat under the lights. His interviewer asked about the work of the Baptist Student Union and about the Help Team. He mentioned his "conversion to Christ" and the interviewer, following that lead, asked, "What do you mean by "conversion to Christ?'"

Tom answered, "I was converted to Christ, that is, I became a Christian when I asked Christ to enter my life. It's more than knowing *about* Jesus Christ. I had to admit my sin and need for God. Because of the death and resurrection of Christ, I was forgiven, and now I have a personal relationship with God."

Tom paused for a breath. The crew was signaling time, so the interviewer said, "Thank you very much, Tom Jackson, for joining us on *Religion Today*." The camera switched back to the news anchor.

Outside we congratulated Tom, and John patted him on the back.

The next day, I skipped class to visit Temple Square in Salt Lake City with the Help Team. We had a look into the Mormon Tabernacle, the home of the famous Choir, and took a guided tour of the grounds. The guides told us the story of Joseph Smith, the angels Moroni and Mormon, Christ's visit to the Americas, and the restoration of the True Church, the same story I'd first heard at Sheryl's ward in Phoenix.

Ann whispered to me, "This sounds like a fairy tale!"

"But that's because you already know a lot about the Bible. The Mormons explain why many Christian churches are dry and dead—because the True Church ended when the last apostle died. If dry, dead religion had been your experience, it would make a lot of sense to you."

As a result of the Help Team visit, several international students showed up at Bible study, and our numbers grew. Dawnena started a monthly BSU newsletter. I got better at delegating responsibilities, which lightened my load and spread out the feeling of ownership among the students. Nancy and Jane, the two freshmen, were happy to get involved. I felt confident that the BSU wouldn't depend on me for survival.

Toward the end of the semester I answered a knock on our door to see young two men dressed in dark suits, stiffly-pressed white shirts, ties, polished shoes, and backpacks. Before they said a word, I knew who they were. One said, "We'd like to speak with Carol Avery."

"I'm Carol. You must be the new missionaries on campus." In the *Daily Universe* I'd read that for the first time, a team of full-time missionaries had been assigned to proselytize the non-members at BYU. Starting with the president of the Baptist Student Union, it looked like.

"Yes, we are. May we come in?"

I offered the men seats in the kitchen. When my roommate Becky glanced in, her eyes got round and she gave me a big smile. Of course, the elders invited me to begin the discussions.

My first ill-fated encounter with the missionaries had left me stinging, but I wasn't scared of missionaries anymore. Thanks to the LDS motto, "every member a missionary" I was pretty sure I had heard all there was to hear already. My friends still regularly challenged me to take the lessons, feeling sure that a trip through the lessons would put the finishing touch on my search for truth. Maybe they were right, actually. It would at least put the finishing touches on my BYU education, and put to rest any final doubts I had. If I could make it through the lessons without converting, I was home free. "Right now I have to get through finals," I said, "but I'm going to stay here during the spring quarter. Why don't you come back and see me then?"

chapter nine

Janet, Becky, and I were staying around for spring term (the first summer session), but our building in Heritage Halls was reserved for missionaries coming to study at the Language Training Mission. We had to leave the apartment immaculate, so during exams, we packed up and scrubbed the apartment, and moved into another building in Heritage Halls. The housing authority assigned us two additional roommates; one was a Japanese Latter-day Saint on her first trip to America.

Victor was finally graduating and going back to Liberia, so the church threw a farewell party for him. Liz was going to Hong Kong for the summer. She still hadn't given in to religion, but it seemed to the rest of us that Christianity had rubbed off on her. Dawn was going home to North Carolina to work for the summer. She had agreed to take her turn as the BSU president in the fall. I wasn't sure I'd be back, so we said our goodbyes and promised to keep in touch, just in case. Sheryl went home to Phoenix, and I knew I'd see her there.

Summertime in Provo was glorious. The BSU wasn't busy, so I had more free time. We studied outdoors and packed picnics. I took a tennis class and a class in Spanish culture.

One afternoon on my way back from class, Becky met me at the door and said, "Oh Carol, the Mission Mormonaries came by to see you."

"Who?"

"The Mission Mormonaries from the Church of Cheese and Crackers of Rattle-day Snakes." She laughed. "When my brother was on his mission we used to call him that."

"Wow. What did they say?"

"They'll call you."

Sure enough, that evening the phone rang. "Carol, this is Elder Smith. Is there anything we can do for you today?"

"I don't think so."

Elder Smith's voice was friendly and assertive. "Carol, we'd like to begin the discussions about the Church with you. Are you free tomorrow?"

We arranged to meet at noon. I was enthusiastic, and only a little apprehensive. For me it was, in a sense, after the fact. I had already sincerely asked God if the Church was true, and I hadn't gotten the burning in the bosom.

Promptly at noon the next day, the dark-suited elders arrived. Elder Smith had the classic Mormon look: blond hair, blue eyes, tall and trim. He looked like he wouldn't be caught dead wearing the nerdy glasses that Elder Richards was wearing. At first I thought Elder Richards had freckles, but a second glance revealed that he was recovering from adolescent acne. Elder Smith evoked my respect and Elder Richards my compassion.

I shook Elder Smith's warm strong hand and Elder Richards's cool damp hand, and we sat down on the green vinyl sofas in the lobby. Elder Smith asked me again if there was anything they could do for me today, and I still couldn't think of anything. I did ask where they were from. Elder Smith was from a small town in southern Utah.

"Do you get home once in a while?" I asked.

"Oh, no. I might as well be on the other side of the world. I do write home once a week."

Elder Richards was from California.

"Southern or Northern?" I asked.

"Northern."

I told him about the band's trip to Oakland and Berkeley last year.

"Oh," he said.

We began lesson one. Supplementing their presentation with a notebook pulled from a backpack, the elders took turns explaining the restoration of the Church and the testimony of Joseph Smith.

As Elder Smith explained the importance of prophets in the Old Testament, he asked, "Carol, why do you feel it would be helpful for God to give us direction and help today?"

I said, "I guess most of us would like direction from God."

"That's right, Carol, and our message and testimony to you is that God continues to guide His children today through living prophets. Our church is organized with apostles and prophets as directed in Ephesians Chapter Four." He had me read Ephesians 4:11 from his King James Bible: "And He Himself gave some to be apostles, some prophets, some evangelists, and some pastors and teachers..."

Then Elder Richards handed me a pamphlet containing the testimony of Joseph Smith. He said that Christ told Joseph in a vision to join none of the churches, for they all taught the doctrines of men and not of God. Then he asked me, "Does this help you understand why the churches today teach so many conflicting doctrines?"

I am sure I was supposed to say yes, but I said, "Christian churches that follow the Bible don't teach many conflicting doctrines. They agree on the major doctrines of the faith."

Elder Richards looked at Elder Smith like a player looks at his coach on the sideline. Elder Smith jumped in and explained that the Book of Mormon is God's gift to us, given to clarify and add to the Bible.

At the end of the lesson, Elder Richards reviewed the concepts we'd studied. He asked, "How do you feel that knowing there is a living prophet on the earth today will help your family?" and then "Can you accept the fact that Joseph Smith received from an angel the gold plates on which the Book of Mormon was written?"

It was only my first lesson, and I wasn't trying to be contrary, but I had to say, "No, I can't accept that."

Elder Smith promised me that I could know for certain the truth of these things through sincere prayer. Elder Richards explained to me how to pray, beginning with "Our Father in Heaven," thanking Him for blessings, asking for what I needed, and closing in the name of Jesus Christ. The men got on their knees right in the lobby and asked me to lead in a closing prayer. After another round of handshakes, they urged me to do my homework: I was to study the pamphlet about Joseph Smith and look up several passages in the Book of Mormon.

During the week I studied diligently. I was finally reading the Book of Mormon. It read like the King James Bible, but heavy on the phrase "and it came to pass." In 3 Nephi I even bumped into the Book of Mormon version of the Sermon on the Mount.

The next week, the elders taught me about eternal progression: we had lived in heaven before we became mortals on earth, and we are here now to obtain bodies of flesh and bone and to be tested. The famous couplet, "As man is, God once was; as God is, man may become" was another important aspect of eternal progression. Again, Elder Richards invited me to pray at the end of the lesson and assured me that God would show me the truth of these things if I asked sincerely. As always, we concluded with handshakes all around.

My heart was tender toward these fine elders, and I impulsively asked, "Would you like to have dinner with my roommates and me next week?"

They exchanged glances, and Elder Smith said, "We'd love to!"

We changed our meeting time to four o'clock, with dinner at five. When I told my roommates, they clapped with delight. Becky said, "Oh Carol, what a privilege it will be to share a meal with them! Can I help you cook?"

So on Thursday we fixed enchiladas, sticking precisely to the recipe from *The Joy of Cooking*. I left Becky to watch the oven and make a salad during my lesson.

Our topic was "continuing revelation" to the Church of Jesus Christ through the Prophet and Apostles. The Latter-day Scriptures: the Book of Mormon, the Doctrine and

Covenants, and the Pearl of Great Price, were also sources of revelation. With great conviction, Elders Smith and Richards taught me that all authority and knowledge necessary for salvation is found in the Church of Jesus Christ, and they emphasized the importance of obedience to Church leaders.

About the tenth time that Elder Smith called it "the Church of Jesus Christ," I spoke up. "Stop. You keep leaving off 'of Latter-day Saints.' I'm already a member of the Church of Jesus Christ. I wish you wouldn't call your church 'the Church of Jesus Christ'."

The elders looked at each other in silence. Elder Smith suppressed a smile.

I finally said, "Go ahead with the lesson."

He picked up where he left off in the notebook. He and Elder Richards did try to use the full name of the Church after that.

When the lesson ended, we borrowed a couple of chairs from a neighbor and crowded in cozily around the kitchen table for dinner. The enchiladas were a little heavy on the onions, but it didn't matter. My roommates rose to the occasion, engaging even shy Elder Richards in conversation. They understood better than I did what topics are fair game to discuss with missionaries and which are off limits. After a light-hearted hour together, the elders left for an evening appointment. Becky helped me with the

dishes. "It's a good thing we cooked a double batch of enchiladas. Those guys were hungry!"

"I'm so honored that we could share a meal with
them. Oh Carol, you're so lucky to be taking the discussions with those elders. Are you learning a lot?"

"I'm no 'golden contact' anymore. I knew most of
this stuff already, but I am having a good time with them."

"I hope you take their teaching seriously."

Janet walked in carrying the mail. "Hey Carol,
here's a letter from North Texas State."

With shaky fingers I tore into the envelope to find
an offer of a modest academic scholarship. The important
part was the waiver included for out-of-state tuition.

"What does it say?" Janet and Becky had waited
eagerly while I read it.

I told them and Janet asked, "What are you going
to do?"

"I don't know. I guess I'd better decide." I put the
letter away and didn't tell anyone else about it yet. It was a
great relief to have the offer, but now that I had it, did I
really want to accept it? Did I really want to leave this beautiful, challenging place?

I sometimes wondered what life would be like at a
"normal" university. And I wasn't sure I wanted to spend
the rest of my life explaining to everyone who saw my re-

sume that I wasn't Mormon in spite of my degree from BYU. But were those reasons enough to leave?

Probably not, but those religion classes were a big problem. Rules were rules, and the university wasn't going to bend them for me just because I didn't like their religion classes. And I was sure that no matter how much I liked it here, or how great the ministry was, all those religion classes were more than reason enough. I signed the acceptance form for North Texas State. Before I mailed it, I called Diane and told her about my decision.

She said, "Carol, I'm not surprised. I hate to see you go, but I know you're doing your best to find God's will for your life. Have fun in Texas."

I also stopped in to tell my favorite professor, Brother Turner, about my scholarship. He congratulated me and said he'd miss me.

"I'll miss you, too. You are one of my favorite people here!" I said. I also mentioned that I was taking the missionary lessons.

"What are you doing that for?"

I was surprised at his sharp tone. "People have been after me for two years to do it, and I figured it's about time."

"Those lessons are designed to lead investigators into the Church. Don't forget that curiosity killed the cat." I sure liked Brother Turner.

The fourth missionary lesson was about truth versus error and taught that God's truth all but disappeared from the earth after the last apostle died. As always, there were verses from the Bible to support this. The elders pointed me to 2 Timothy 4:3-4: "For the time will come when they will not endure sound doctrine; but after their own lusts shall they heap to themselves teachers, having itching ears; and they shall turn away their ears from the truth, and shall be turned unto fables" (KJV).

I said, "How do you know this verse isn't talking about you? Maybe it is the Mormons who have turned aside to fables, not me."

"Carol, we're not talking about you personally!" Elder Smith laughed and then returned to the script. "We believe God came and restored the Church through Joseph Smith because man had gone astray, and the True Church was lost from the earth." I decided not to remind them of Jesus' promise that the gates of hell would not prevail against his church.

Elder Smith continued to guide the discussion. "By the way, Carol, how do you feel about Joseph Smith's vision?"

"Not good. I don't think God appeared to Joseph Smith. The Bible says that God is spirit, and that no one has seen God."

He said, "You don't still believe in the three-in-one

doctrine, do you?"

"In the Trinity? Yes, I do."

Poor Elder Smith. After four lessons he hadn't even convinced me that God the Father had a body of flesh and bone. "Oh Carol, haven't you seen all those verses about the face of God and His arms and hands? Don't you know God created man in His own image? And tell me, how could Jesus be a man on earth and be God in heaven at the same time? If Jesus was God, how could God pray to Himself?"

"I can show you verses that say God is spirit and that no man can see God. And I can show you that the Bible says Jesus was God."

"Carol, what can we do to help you see that God is not three-in-one?"

"Nothing I can think of."

He passed the notebook on to Elder Richards who explained the LDS plan of salvation. The first point, "faith," was refreshingly common ground. We both believed in the importance of faith—though our definitions of the word were different. We did well on the second point of salvation too, "repentance," until he said that after repentance, if we ever committed the same sin, the repentance was invalid.

The third point of salvation was baptism, which he said was essential to salvation. And the next was that after a new convert is baptized, the missionaries lay hands on him or her and bestow the gift of the Holy Ghost.

"How can a person give the gift of the Holy Spirit? Only God Himself can," I said, trying not to be belligerent, but also determined to not be carried away by sketchy reasoning.

"Do you feel the gift of the Holy Ghost is a blessing worth working for?"

"Worth working for?" I was baffled. "How can you work for a gift? You just said the Holy Ghost is a gift."

"Actually, the fifth point of salvation, or exaltation, is enduring to the end. It's a gift, but what we do with the gift matters. We are to practice the ordinances and obey the laws of the Church till we die. We believe that we are saved by grace, after all that we can do. So works are an important part of completing our salvation."

The elders went on to finish the lesson with the topic of goals. After challenging me to set goals in my personal life, Elder Richards suggested a specific date at the end of the month by which I should know for certain the truth of the Church. I noticed later that the date was a Saturday, the day baptisms were held.

I dropped by Brother Turner's office again. "How are your missionary lessons going?" he asked.

"It's a challenge for all of us."

"How's that?"

"The elders get frustrated because I don't accept

their most elementary points. I'm not trying to be obnoxious, but I can't say I agree with them when I really don't. And all those leading questions are irritating, like 'Do you feel it was important for Joseph Smith to receive proper authority before establishing the Church in the Lord's name?' and 'Do you suppose we would have to develop faith to remember what it was like to be in the premortal existence with God?'"

"I see." He stared at the ceiling for a while, then spoke. "I joined the Church after missionary age so I never served a full-time mission, but I've been a stake missionary. I always tried to beef up the lessons since I wanted to present a complete picture of the Church, not just convince people to join. I think the direction of the lessons can be misleading. I didn't baptize very many converts."

"Wow. Thanks for sharing that." I greatly respected Brother Turner for his honest heart.

Lesson five was about obeying the commandments. "The commandments," Elder Smith sermonized, "are given to show us how to achieve eternal life and become like God."

First was the law of tithing. Although I didn't consider tithing a "law," when I told the elders that as a Baptist I already practiced tithing, they were astonished and praised my good works.

It fell upon Elder Richard to talk about the law of chastity. He began by talking about the sacred power God has given us to create life.

"I agree with the law of chastity," I said.

"Good." Elder Richards relaxed, and he quickly went on to the next commandment, the Word of Wisdom. He asked me whether I used tobacco, alcohol, coffee, or tea.

I said, "I signed the Honor Code. I don't drink, smoke, or even like coffee anyway."

He preached a short sermon on the harmful effects of caffeine, and said, "You're fortunate to be surrounded by others who maintain the Word of Wisdom."

The last point of obedience was keeping the Sabbath. Elder Smith exhorted me to attend my branch meetings.

By the end of this lesson, it was clear to me that Mormons and Christians did many of the same things for different reasons. Latter-day Saints obeyed commandments to earn favor in God's sight and obtain exaltation. But I, as a Baptist, had been taught to obey God out of gratitude, knowing that we can't earn salvation on our own.

Meanwhile, at the First Baptist Church, Pastor Phil McKown had started an evangelism training program for church members. Our homework assignment was to present the "Four Spiritual Laws" booklet to several friends. This booklet explained the Christian plan of salvation in four simple steps: God's love for people, our sin, Christ's death as the only remedy for our sin, and our need to respond individually to Christ's offer of salvation.

My first subject was Becky, who listened patiently to my presentation. When I asked the final question about who was on the "throne" of her life, herself or Christ, Becky indicated that Christ was indeed in charge of her life.

At the end, I asked Becky her opinion of the booklet. She said, "The Bible says that faith without works is dead."

"I know. But I think it means that unless our faith produces good works, it isn't true faith. It is dead."

Becky insisted that God's grace could be earned. I said, "No, the Bible teaches that salvation can't be earned."

It was getting heated, but I really liked Becky and I didn't want to argue—with her especially; she had sympathized with me so nicely about family prayer last fall. I said, "Well, at least now you know what I believe. Thanks for listening."

"Yeah," she said. "I guess you hear what we believe all the time."

Later, as Janet finished washing dishes. I said, "Janet, can you help me? I'm taking this class at church, and for homework we are supposed to present this little booklet to several people. Would you be able to listen to me for a few minutes?"

She dried her hands with a towel, and sat down at the table, arms folded tightly, mouth grim. As I read through the booklet, if she agreed with a point, she said, "true" and if she didn't agree, she was silent. When we finished, she said nothing.

"Thanks for listening, Janet." I gave her the booklet, but she left it in the kitchen. The apartment went icy for a while, but in a few days the chill melted, and we were back to our usual, if odd, friendship.

My next customers were the elders. I went to my last lesson with the tracts in my pocket. The first topic was the person of Jesus Christ.

Elder Smith talked about man's need for a savior, and quoted, "for all have sinned and fall short of the glory of God." He stopped, looked at Elder Richards, and whispered, "Where's that verse—in Romans?"

Elder Richards drew a blank, too.

"You mean Romans 3:23," I said.

Both elders, who were thumbing through their Bibles, turned quickly there.

"You're right!" Elder Smith conceded. "You should be a missionary."

"Maybe I already am!"

We went on to the last topic about our responsibility as members of the kingdom. This was a checklist for baptism.

"So Carol," Elder Smith said, "You've been a diligent student with your homework. Have you been praying that God would show you the truth?"

"I have, and he has. You guys did a great job teaching me these lessons, but I'm not a candidate for baptism. Sorry." Then I said, "May I take a couple of minutes to tell you what I believe?"

The elders looked at each other in surprise. "I suppose it would be only fair," said Elder Richards.

I handed each one a copy of the "Four Spiritual Laws" and read it aloud, trying to make my voice sound casual.

We came to that question about who was on the throne of their lives, themselves or Christ. Both men, without a moment's hesitation, said, "My life is directed by Jesus Christ."

Then I realized, of course that's their answer. These dear guys were doing everything they knew to please God and obey Him, and so were my roommates. They were following God as they understood Him with every "bone and fiber of their beings." They just didn't understand salvation by grace the way I did.

When I finished the booklet, the elders were eager to express their opinions.

"Most of this is true," said Elder Smith, "but it should be carried a step further. Faith is fine, but to obtain perfection we must follow the commandments."

"Besides," said Elder Richards, "they left out the restoration of the Church!"

We all laughed.

A couple weeks later, Elder Smith called. As usual, he asked if there was anything he could do for me and said he had a cassette tape to loan to me. He also mentioned that Diane Cross was going to take the lessons too.

"She is?" Diane had thought it was a bad idea for me to take the lessons, but she had listened with great interest to my weekly reports about them. I was eager to congratulate Diane for her courage.

Finally, with a twinkle in his voice, he asked, "Would you like me to heat up the baptismal waters for you?"

"No, *thanks!*" I replied with a laugh.

Janet had finished corresponding with her missionary in Germany. Now, of course, being surrounded by returned missionaries, she had been asked out now and then. She sometimes confided in me, wondering aloud, "Could this be 'The One'?"

This summer's suitor, Gary, was a dashing fellow who treated Janet and all of us with elegance. He was a frequent dinner guest and even took us for rides on the back of his motorcycle.

One night after dessert, Gary said, "I'd like to make a proposal." He whipped something out of his pocket and slipped it on Janet's finger. We laughed, and then we saw it really was a diamond ring, and Gary was serious. Becky shrieked and threw her arms around Janet's neck. I ran for the camera.

Janet said yes, right on the spot. I hugged her. Janet's life dream—marriage and family—was coming true. That autumn, Janet and Gary were married in the temple. Janet had become a beloved friend. I couldn't have been happier for her. I was sorry I wasn't allowed to attend the temple wedding, but at least I was there for the proposal.

I wondered whether I'd get a chance to say goodbye to my clarinet-playing friend David. I wasn't about to call him up, though I had heard he was still around for the summer. Sure enough, one day I stepped into an elevator in the fine arts building to find myself facing him.

"Hi," we chimed in unison.

"I haven't seen you in a long time," David said.

"I'm leaving soon. I decided to transfer to North Texas State University."

"Oh, I didn't know that," he said softly.

"It's true. I'm really leaving."

"We'll miss you. Sharon will have to blow twice as loud in the orchestra."

"Yeah." I smiled at the thought.

The elevator had carried us to the third floor by now, and the door opened. I reached out to prevent it from closing and said, "David, I'm glad I got to know you. You were a good friend."

"Thanks, Carol. I respect you greatly, more than you'll ever know. I'm sure you'll be successful in whatever you do." He gave me a long, proper Mormon handshake. The elevator kept trying to close on my other hand.

"Bye, David." I stepped out slowly.

"Goodbye, Carol," he said. We watched the door close between us.

I sighed deeply and prayed, "Lord, I'm glad you're with me."

As I reached the end of two years in Utah, I wanted to leave a legacy for the Baptist Student Union. I organized all the materials and ideas I'd accumulated in a notebook for Dawnena, including a special page of wacky suggestions for her.

Pastor Phil McKown had arranged with administrators at BYU to obtain the roster of Baptist students during the summer. We planned a BSU retreat before registration and wrote letters inviting new students to attend. On my last Sunday at First Baptist, the church members threw me a farewell and thank-you reception with dessert, a gift, and hugs and kind words all around.

With Phil, Diane, and Dawnena working together, I was sure the BSU would thrive without me. And it warmed my heart to consider how far we'd already come. Who would have thought, two years ago, that we'd host a convention, enter a float in the homecoming parade, hand out Bibles on campus, and become so well-known that recruiters would brag about us?

My father arrived from Phoenix, and we loaded the station wagon back up. Two years ago, I had cried when Dad left me here. Now I was crying about leaving BYU behind. I took Dad on one last walk around the beautiful campus together as story after story tumbled out into his listening ears.

"Well, daughter, you kept the faith, didn't you?" my dad said.

"Yes, Dad, I did."

epilogue

*D*iane Cross directed the Baptist Student Union until 1982, when she went to Golden Gate Theological Seminary to teach and do advanced studies. For the past nine years, a BYU teacher has been the faculty advisor of the BSU, which still reaches out to students on campus who are interested in being part of a born-again Christian group.

About sixty people regularly attend the First Baptist Church of Provo, many of whom, including the pastor himself, are former Mormons.

Dawnena graduated from BYU and after a year in New Mexico raising funds for Native American scholarships she returned to North Carolina to open the first Travel and Promotion Office for her tribe of Cherokee Indians. She got married in 1980, and has one daughter.

June and Gary continue as faithful Latter-day Saints. Gary has been the bishop of his ward, and June, the mother of four children, has been the Relief Society President of her ward for many years.

Sheryl married Mark, and they settled down to teach music in southern Utah. She is the mother of seven children and became a grandmother at age 42.

I graduated from the University of North Texas in 1978. After teaching music, Spanish, and English in Texas, Colorado, the Dominican Republic, and China, I married Ron Forseth in 1988. After finishing graduate degrees in English we spent most of the 1990's teaching English in China and Mongolia with our children Rachel and Randy.

I first wrote this story soon after I left Brigham Young University, and it was published as *Faith Under Fire* in 1989. I revised it because now I am (a) a better writer and (b) less of a know-it-all.

After much consideration, I changed the names of most of my LDS friends mentioned in this book. I wouldn't want any of my old friends or professors to be called to task by their Church for their words or deeds as I've remembered them.

As for terminology, the official Church media statement prefers the use of the full name "the Church of Jesus Christ of Latter-day Saints," shortened when necessary to "the Church of Jesus Christ." This can be cumbersome or ambiguous, and Church members do refer to themselves as LDS, and their Church as the LDS Church. Using the term "Mormons" to refer to Church members is officially acceptable as well, as is the term "Mormonism" when describing the culture and lifestyle of the Church.

I am indebted to Richard Ostling and Joan Ostling, the authors of *Mormon America*, for current information and for their compassionate, balanced perspective about the Church of Jesus Christ of Latter-day Saints.

My next book is a firsthand chronicle of the Great Depression of the 1990's in Outer Mongolia.

Appendix A

The Bible and Mormon Doctrine

---

*A*s promised, here is the list from the back of Pastor Don Plott's Bible, with additions. Latter-day Saints don't accept the Bible as their final authority, so the following verses don't "prove" anything to them. Because of the principle of continuing revelation, if the Bible interferes with modern teaching, the new supersedes the old. But for Christians who want to compare what the Bible says with LDS doctrine, the following verses may be helpful.

- God is spirit: John 4:24.
- There is only one God: Deuteronomy 6:4, 32:39, Deuteronomy 13:1-3, Isaiah 44:6-8.

- God is not a man: Numbers 23:19, Hosea 11:9.
- No man can see God: Exodus 33:20, John 1:18, 1 Timothy 6:13-16, 1 John 4:12, Colossians 1:15.
- God does not change or progress: 1 Samuel 15:29, Malachi 3:6, James 1:17.
- God no longer dwells in temples made with human hands: Acts 7:48, Acts 17:24, Revelation 21:22.
- God the Father and Jesus are One (the Trinity): John 1:1-2, John 10:30, John 14:16-20, John 14:23, Philippians 2:6, Colossians 2:8-9, 2 Peter 1:1.
- We are not saved by works: Romans 3:28, Galatians 2:16-3:25, Ephesians 2:8-9, Colossians 2:16-23, Titus 3:5-6.
- There is no second chance after death: Hebrews 9:27.
- There is no pre-mortal existence: Genesis 2:7, Psalm 139:13-16, 1 Corinthians 15:46.
- The Bible is to be unaltered: Proverbs 30:5-6, Isaiah 40:8, Revelation 22:18-19.
- There is no marriage in heaven: Matthew 22:30, Mark 12:25, Luke 20:34-35, Romans 7:1-2.
- Old Testament-style prophets are no longer necessary because Jesus has come: Matthew 11:13, Luke 16:16, Hebrews 1:1-2.
- Ministers may receive compensation: 1 Corinthians 9:1-23, 1 Timothy 5:17-18.
- Warnings against another gospel: 2 Corinthians 11:4, Galatians 1:6-9, 1 Timothy 1:3.

Appendix B

What to do About Your LDS Friends

*B*ack in the old days, Latter-day Saints huddled in Utah and Idaho to escape persecution and set up their own theocracy. But in this new era, Latter-day Saints are scattered far and wide across the nation and the world. They are our neighbors, employers, clients, teachers, and congressmen. Our kids attend school and play soccer together. We're in aerobics classes together. We play golf together.

And Latter-day Saints share common ground, especially politically and morally, with traditional Christians. We're all doing the best we can to keep our country great and to raise our kids right. But we don't see eye-to-eye on all matters of faith. If you are an Evangelical Christian, you may want your LDS friend to see the light, while he or she wants you to see the light of the "restored gospel." It's a conflict of interests right from the start.

Speaking of Christianity, people often ask, "Aren't Mormons Christians?" After all, it is called the Church of Jesus Christ of Latter-day Saints. Mormons do pray "in the name of Jesus Christ." And the Book of Mormon does carry the subtitle "Another Testament of Jesus Christ."

The Saints claim, in fact, not only to be Christians, but also to be the only true Christians, members of the only true Church of Jesus Christ on earth. LDS Scriptures deny the legitimacy of every other church and reject essential Christian doctrines about God, Jesus Christ, sin, salvation, and the authority of the Bible. But being a Christian, in my thinking, is less about what church a person joins and more about the condition of one's heart and soul in relation to Jesus Christ. Given that, some Mormons who have believed solely in Jesus might in fact be Christians, and some Baptists might not.

But rather than spend your energy debating that point, just be thankful if you have the privilege of befriending a Mormon, many of whom don't even have close friends outside the Church. The best gifts you can give your LDS friends are understanding and love.

Understand Them

Mormonism is much more than a religion; it's a way of life. The LDS Church offers a ready-made social community all over the world, unparalleled support for families, moral teaching to keep children on the straight and narrow path, a romanticized history, a healthy lifestyle, enrichment through quilting classes and Boy Scouts, and answers to life's difficult questions.

In general, Latter-day Saints take their history and doctrine by faith, or more accurately, by feeling. They know in their *hearts* that the Church is true, and they invite investigators to seek a "burning in the bosom" to verify the truth of the Church.

Latter-day Saints aren't Saints because of the historical authenticity of their Scriptures. Typically, they don't worry about what the Smithsonian Institution has said about the Book of Mormon. They don't want to know every detail about Joseph Smith's and Brigham Young's personal lives. Mormons like what their Church has to offer and don't want to listen to damaging information about it. As Apostle Boyd K. Packer said in a famous speech to Church educators, "Some things that are true are not very useful."

There are, however, and have been since the beginning, Latter-day Saints willing to make the break from the Church. For instance, each of the Three Witnesses, whose testimony is printed in the front of every Book of Mormon, eventually left the Church. And in recent years, several high-profile Saints have been excommunicated from the Church for speaking out or writing on matters of historical authenticity or controversial topics such as feminism and Church repression of information. Others have quit the church in protest.

The Latter-day Saint equivalent of the "backslidden Baptist" or the "non-practicing" Jew or Catholic is the "Jack Mormon." Jack or Jackie may be a convert who found out disappointing things about the Church after being baptized. Or he or she may be a born-and-bred cultural Mormon who just can't take all the control.

So you might meet a Mormon who is open to spiritual truth from outside the LDS Church. If and when you "talk religion" with your LDS friend, remember:

- To Latter-day Saints, the Bible is not authoritative; it is the only Standard Work that contains errors. You can't "prove" anything with the Bible. You can, of course, let the Bible speak for itself. Only the King James Version (or Joseph Smith's Inspired Version) is acceptable to a practicing Mormon. To use any other translation is to create another obstacle.

- Latter-day Saints do not see themselves as "lost." In fact, they not only have Christ but also the "fullness of the restored gospel." They have been taught to obtain exaltation by their own good efforts (though many would sincerely add, "with God's help").

- Latter-day Saints live under a strong hierarchy that doesn't invite independent reasoning about religious matters.

- Latter-day Saints use the same religious words as orthodox Christians (such as salvation, heaven, and gospel) but the meanings are often different. There are vast differences between the LDS and Christian concepts of God, Christ, and salvation.

- Leaving the Church is extremely hard on the psyche of long-time Mormons. The heavily trafficked online support site, exmormon.org, is dedicated to helping former Mormons through the trauma of leaving the Church. The site has no religious affiliation but helps Mormons regain control of their own thinking.

• A Christian's goal is not to help Mormons out of their Church; rather it is to share the good news about grace through faith in the Jesus of the Bible.

Love Them

Christians are called to live humbly as a light among the people around them, and it's a gift from God if some of those people are LDS. In those relationships, let the love of Christ control you, rather than fear or hostility. It is not a compromise of truth to love an LDS friend. And your godliness and grace will penetrate hearts far more effectively brash argumentation ever will.

By the way, the Mormon missionaries who come to your door are worthy of kindness and love, but it's nearly impossible to build a friendship with them. They aren't allowed to be out of sight or hearing of their companions, and if one of them shows signs of doubt or weakness, he or she will be transferred to another site. They spend more than six days a week, twelve hours a day, preaching their faith. There's no room for doubt in a missionary's life. But Christ Himself would invite them inside to thaw out for a few minutes on a cold day or offer them a cup of cold water (not tea!) on a hot day.

Keep the anti-Mormon literature to yourself; some of it is inflammatory, offensive, and hard for a Mormon to understand anyway. Read it yourself and be able to discuss the concepts with your friend.

Some good advice for relating to Mormons is found in 2 Timothy 2:23-26 (NIV):

> "Don't have anything to do with foolish and stupid arguments, because you know they produce quarrels. And the Lord's servant must not quarrel; instead, he must be kind to everyone, able to teach, not resentful. Those who oppose him he must gently instruct, in the hope that God will grant them repentance leading them to a knowledge of the truth, and that they will come to their senses and escape from the trap of the devil, who has taken them captive to do his will."

When any person, Mormon or otherwise, comes to personal faith in Jesus Christ, it is a work of God. So above all pray for your LDS friends. As Jesus said, "No one can come to me unless the Father who sent me draws him" (John 6:44, NIV).

Appendix C

Sources for Additional Information

Latter-day Saint Sources

1999-2000 *Church Almanac*. Salt Lake City: *Deseret News*, 1998. Every two years the LDS-owned daily newspaper publishes an almanac with official statistics about Church membership, temples, missions, and biographies of past and present General Authorities of the Church.

McConkie, Bruce R. *Mormon Doctrine* (2nd edition). Salt Lake City: Bookcraft, 1979. Mormon doctrine as defined by an LDS apostle. This book is widely studied and quoted within the LDS Church.

Official web site of the Church of Jesus Christ of Latter-day Saints: *www.lds.org*. I am indebted to this site for reliable and current information about the LDS Church.

Official web site of Brigham Young University: *www.byu.edu*. I took sweet trips down this memory lane viewing photographs of the campus and former professors.

The Scholarly and Historical Information Exchange for Latter-day Saints (SHIELDS) and the Foundation for Apologetic Information and Research (FAIR): *www.shields-research.org* and *www.fair-lds.org*. The mission of these two LDS organizations (recently merged) is to defend the Church of Jesus Christ of Latter-day Saints against its critics. Information about various critics is posted on the site.

Foundation for Ancient Research and Mormon Studies: *www.farms.byu.edu*. FARMS is a nonprofit educational foundation at Brigham Young University that encourages and supports research about the Book of Mormon.

Other Sources

Ostling, Richard N. and Joan K. *Mormon America*. San Francisco: HarperSanFrancisco, 1999. A comprehensive, compassionate look at Mormonism's history, beliefs, culture, and power structure, written by Protestant journalists. *Mormon America* is certain to be a definitive work for years to come.

Tanner, Jerald and Sandra. *Mormonism—Shadow or Reality?* Utah Lighthouse Ministry, 1987. This is the most famous of hundreds of resources available from Utah's most famous former Mormons. The Tanners also print copies of the original 1830 Book of Mormon in which they have marked 3,913 of the changes made. The Tanners' web site follows.

Utah Lighthouse Ministry: *www.utlm.org*. Jerald and Sandra Tanner were raised in the LDS faith, both with a family history that can be traced to the patriarchs of the Church. Now ex-Mormon Christians, the Tanners have dedicated their lives to publishing objective material that disputes the claims of the LDS Church. Links on this site can put you through to most any other ministry to Mormons, and most any book about Mormonism can be purchased through their virtual bookstore.

Mormons in Transition: *www.irr.org/mit*. Mormons in Transition, sponsored by the non-denominational Christian Institute for Religious Research, provides a support group and volumes of information for Mormons and former Mormons questioning their faith.

Mormonism Research Ministry: *www.mrm.org*. Bill McKeever founded Mormonism Research Ministry in 1979 with the goal of informing the Body of Christ about the differences between Mormonism and Christianity and reaching out to members of the LDS Church.

Saints Alive in Jesus: *www.saintsalive.com*. Ed Decker, a former Mormon, is the founder of Saints Alive in Jesus and author of the controversial book and film about Mormonism, *The God Makers*. Saints Alive is one of the more forceful critics of the LDS Church.

Recovery from Mormonism: *www.exmormon.org*. This web site provides a support group for former members and those questioning their faith in the Church of Jesus Christ of Latter-day Saints. The site offers e-groups, bulletin boards, and a significant collection of stories of former Mormons. It advocates no specific religious preference after Mormonism.

To order copies of *Gentile Girl* or to contact the author, log on to *www.gentilegirl.com*.

Mailing Address:
Crossroads Press
P.O Box 272817
Fort Collins, CO 80527-2817

Fax: 815-352-1280

Include shipping address and telephone number, a check for total number of books ($11.95 U.S. each) and $3.00 shipping and handling (for the first book, $1 S & H per additional book). For quantity orders, contact Crossroads Press at *info@gentilegirl.com*.

epilogue

[1] The LTM (Language Training Mission) has been replaced by the MTC (Missionary Training Center) where both foreign and domestic LDS missionaries receive training prior to their two-year missions.

[2] The Relief Society is one of the oldest and largest women's organizations in the world. It was established in 1842 to help the sick, the poor, and others in need of compassionate service. During its weekly meetings, the organization provides instruction on a variety of topics, including theology, home and family education, compassionate service, social relations, and home management.

[3] General Authorities include the President and his Counselors and the Twelve Apostles of the Church.

[4] His list of Bible verses is Appendix A.

[5] In related LDS theology, Joseph Smith taught that God has a body of flesh and bone (*Doctrine and Covenants* 130:22). Brigham Young taught that Adam was God (*Journal of Discourses,* Volume 1, page 50).

[6] It's not bulletproof underwear. Although there are many Mormon folktales about the sacred garments protecting the wearer

from harm, most Saints wear the garments as a private reminder of their faith and a shared bond with fellow members. It's part of LDS culture and understandably treated with appropriate discretion.

[7] In a revelation announced by Spencer W. Kimball on June 8, 1978, "Every faithful, worthy man in the Church may receive the holy priesthood without regard for race or color." This revelation allowing Blacks to hold the priesthood was perhaps the most historic announcement since 1890 when the Manifesto ending polygamy was issued. Since 1978, the Church has expanded proselytizing efforts in black Africa.

[8] The old Language Training Mission has been replaced by the new Missionary Training Center in Provo.

[9] See the appendix for a list of resources that examine the authenticity of Mormon historical claims.